D0250259

77

No Talent
No Experience
and (almost) No Cost
Businesses
You Can Start Today!

Kelly Reno

PRIMA PUBLISHING

To my husband, Fred,
for his support and love.

Library of Congress Cataloging-in-Publication Data

Reno, Kelly.
    77 no talent, no experience, and (almost) no cost businesses you can start today! / Kelly Reno.
        p.   cm.
    ISBN 0-7615-0246-7
    1. New business enterprises.   2. Small business—Management.   I. Title.
II. Title: Seventy-seven no talent, no experience, and (almost) no cost businesses you can start today!
HD62.5.R44   1995
658.02'2—dc20   95-31323
                                                                 CIP

95 96 97 98 99 DD 10 9 8 7 6 5 4 3 2 1
Printed in the United States of America

Disclaimer: The business ideas and plans presented herein are not a guarantee of financial success. The information is based on experience, research, examples, and advice of entrepreneurs. Publisher and Author assume no liability for any loss or damages that result from applying the information contained in this book. Readers are encouraged to thoroughly research any and all business opportunities before investing their time, energy, and financial resources.

How to Order:

Single copies may be ordered from Prima Publishing, P.O. Box 1260BK, Rocklin, CA 95677; telephone (916) 632-4400. Quantity discounts are also available. On your letterhead, include information concerning the intended use of the books and the number of books you wish to purchase.

CONTENTS

3

Organizing Your New Business   165

4

**Advertising and Promoting
Your Business**

5

Getting Set Up Legally

6

How to Be Your Own Boss

7

Selling Your Business

8

**The Golden Rules of
Professionalism**

INTRODUCTION

Is it still possible to attain financial freedom in this uncertain age of corporate layoffs and skyrocketing unemployment rates? Should we just sit back and consider ourselves fortunate to be holding a dead-end job while making somebody else rich? Is it just a fact of life that most parents can't afford to stay home and raise their families?

Do you recall the old American Dream that you were taught as a youngster? It went something like this: Get an education, get a job, work hard, get promoted, have a family, buy a nice house in a nice neighborhood, take a tropical vacation every few years, and retire in comfort. Okay. Get started! For many of us, though, it didn't quite work out that way and wasn't as easy as we'd figured. Life itself seemed to somehow twist and turn our plans and dreams into a hopeless nightmare of overdue bills, grouchy bosses, broken-down cars, dead-end streets, and financial despair. What went wrong? Is there any way out?

There is, and you'll find answers and a wealth of information within the pages of this book that may very well change your life. By reading the following chapters, you'll discover ways to move from entrapment to entrepreneur. Yes, you can be your own boss by starting a home-based business with little or no money. I've found that the happiest people in the world are those who are living out their dreams and making a living at the same time. You, too, can join these independent and successful business owners.

Let's take the incredible story of Fred R. and Michael D., two adventurous young men who turned a great idea into an extremely lucrative business. Fred had been working as a retail salesman and managed to bring in enough money to pay his bills, yet he always dreamed of owning his own company and really getting ahead in life. Fred's friend, Michael, was an established entrepreneur ready to play a different game and venture into a new field. The two of them put their heads together and thought about what kind of unique service they could provide for the community without spending a fortune to get their business off the ground. After carefully studying and researching the needs of their neighbors, they figured out their new business: Fred and Michael got their permits and tools together and opened the doors of their new chimney sweeping company in just weeks.

In their humble beginnings, they did all of the labor themselves and had only an answering machine to take calls. The two of them worked around the clock, slowly building up a client base. After a typical, grueling day out in the field, Fred and Michael stayed up most of the night at the kitchen table licking stamps and addressing and sealing envelopes for their mailing lists. It wasn't easy, but they were too busy and making too much money to complain. Within a few months they had trained a couple of men to sweep chimneys and had hired several staff members to help out in the office. They *always* spent a large percentage of their income on promotion and marketing, which kept the business booming. The company expanded at a phenomenal rate, while their personal and company bank accounts grew larger each week.

By the end of their first year, the business had already grossed over $1 million! Fred and Michael are living proof that a great idea can become a moneymaking machine with nothing more than hard work, persistence, and imaginative advertising campaigns. After three years and several million dollars, they were ready to move on to bigger and better things. The dynamic duo sold the company to another bright, ambitious man who, in turn, kept expanding it by following the successful actions of his predecessors. The company still exists and has over two hundred employees.

This book is not about getting rich quick. Although that just might happen, as in the case of Fred and Michael, you'll soon find out that starting a business is tough yet rewarding work. In this book you will discover many unique and creative business ideas that can be started on a full- or part-time basis right from your own living room. You'll also find useful information about permits, advertising, organization, and other areas that you might need help with.

If you read, understand, and apply the information in this book, you, too, can achieve financial and personal success in your new business venture. The rewards of owning and operating your own company can be simply spectacular. Isn't it time to start living and to turn that old American Dream into reality?

Vital Research Before You Begin

In this chapter we'll look at the single most important aspect of your new business venture: You. Have you got what it takes to be a success in the exciting and lucrative world of small businesses?

Starting your own company is a major decision, one that can change your life forever. Imagine having a real income from a profession that allows you to control your financial fate. You can be as wealthy as you like, and there will be no bosses or supervisors hanging around to tell you what to do. It takes a tough individual to survive in the business jungle, and only you can guarantee your success. Do you think that you can make it on your own? I'll let you in on a little secret: Your opinion of yourself is the key to success or failure. You can accomplish anything that you can dream of as long as you believe in yourself.

TEST OF SUCCESS

Start by taking the following test. Your answers to these questions will give you some insight on what you think of your own ability to succeed.

True or false:

1. I prefer to take orders rather than give them.
2. I like people.
3. I am able to keep myself on a strict schedule.
4. I truly enjoy working toward goals.
5. I am able to plan and carry out a project.
6. I like working and producing things.
7. I am not willing to take risks.
8. I don't like it when other people tell me what to do.
9. I consider myself to have an optimistic outlook on life.
10. I am responsible and keep my promises.

Multiple choice:

1. If I overslept one morning and was going to be late for an appointment with a customer, I would:
   A. Call the customer and apologize for the inconvenience and do my best to arrive as soon as possible.
   B. Arrive late at the customer's house and offer free service to make up for the inconvenience.
   C. Not waste time by making a phone call, figuring that the customer will understand if I'm late.
   D. Make up a story about having a flat tire or engine trouble.

2. If I had planned a weekend vacation and a customer wanted to schedule a large job that would conflict with my plans, I would:
   A. Tell the customer, "Sorry, but I only work Monday through Friday."
   B. Explain to my traveling companions that I have to work this weekend and must pass on the trip this time.

    C. Figure that I'll probably never have the time to take a vacation anyway and make myself available every day of the year.

    D. Tell the customer that I was unavailable, then provide the phone number of my competition.

3. When my business is going well and I'm starting to get overloaded with appointments, I should:

    A. Stop advertising for more business.

    B. Slow down the advertising until I know that I can handle all of the work.

    C. Continue advertising at full speed and hire and train employees to help me handle all of the business.

    D. Give all of the jobs that I can't handle to a competitor.

4. In starting my new business, I should plan on working:

    A. Approximately 40 to 50 hours a week.

    B. As little as possible as long as I'm able to make a profit.

    C. About 20 hours a week.

    D. As many hours as I can possibly fit into my schedule.

5. If I'm going to make money with my new business, I'll have to:

    A. Be lucky and hope that things go well.

    B. Charge customers a lot of money for my services.

    C. Work hard while charging fair and honest prices.

    D. Sacrifice all of my spare time and slave away like a dog.

Test Scoring:

To score your test, add up the points for each question, which will give you a total number of points. Find out where you score in the evaluation section.

True or false

1. T-0	F-1	6. T-1	F-0
2. T-1	F-0	7. T-0	F-1
3. T-1	F-0	8. T-1	F-0
4. T-1	F-0	9. T-1	F-0
5. T-1	F-0	10. T-1	F-0

Multiple choice

1. A - 4	2. A - 1	3. A - 1	4. A - 3	5. A - 2
B - 2	B - 4	B - 3	B - 1	B - 1
C - 3	C - 2	C - 4	C - 2	C - 4
D - 1	D - 3	D - 2	D - 4	D - 3

Test Evaluation:

30–23 points

You're a natural entrepreneur and undoubtedly have had many successes in your life. You posses a good understanding of responsibility, leadership, and integrity, which will give you that extra edge in operating your business. You are optimistic and willing to work hard to make things go right.

22–16 points

You're definitely on the right track and have a good amount of business savvy under your belt, but could use a little education to perfect what you already know. You strive to be successful, but sometimes find yourself getting into trouble with certain aspects of the game. Try taking the test again after you've read this book.

15 points or below

Don't worry that you scored in the low range. You're already ahead of most people because you're making an effort to better your life by looking into opening your own business. Many a successful business owner started off here and was able to turn things around through hard work and education. Continue reading this book, paying special attention to the chapters on organization and advertising, then take the test again.

WHAT TYPE OF BUSINESS SHOULD I START?

Once you have confidence in your own abilities to start and manage a business, the next step is to take a good, long look at the type of business you'd like to operate. You might find a business idea in this book that interests you or you might dream up one of your own. Either way, put your idea to the test. There are a few important points to research before starting any business that will help you to evaluate and decide if it is the right field for you. Ask yourself these questions about your business idea:

1. Does your new business have the potential to provide you with the kind of income that you'd like to be making?
2. Will you be happy and satisfied doing this type of work, even a few years from now?
3. Are you willing and able to dedicate the time and attention that this type of business requires?
4. Is your service or product something that is needed and wanted in the community?

If your business idea passes the questions above with a definite yes, you may just have found your gold mine. If not, keep researching and looking for another idea until you find one that passes the test with flying colors. If you answer no to any one of these four questions, you could have serious trouble with your company down the road. Take your time and never rush onto the highway until you've carefully mapped out your route.

Great Ideas
for Businesses

In this chapter you will find seventy-seven ideas for businesses that can be started with little or no money or experience. The businesses listed have been the cornerstone of many successful entrepreneurs. Each listing will give you a brief look at the business idea and information that will help you get started. You will also find at the head of each listing an approximate dollar amount to start the business and a basic list of the equipment you will need. (The cost of vehicles, permits, and licenses have not been figured into the dollar amounts because these costs vary from state to state and depend on the type of business.) It is also wise to consult an attorney and accountant prior to embarking on your business venture. See chapter 5, "Getting Set Up Legally," for more information.

The businesses have been chosen and researched carefully and require no special skills or education. Most of the businesses can be started immediately from your own home and can be operated on a full- or part-time schedule.

AIR DUCT CLEANING

Start up cost: $400.

Equipment needed: Ladder, shop vacuum, vacuum brush attachments, duct tape, standard tool kit, droplight, flashlight, garden sprayer (2 gallon), caulking gun, sheet metal cutters, small pieces of sheet metal (used for patches), sheet metal screws, and respirator.

Air ducts are the tubes that hot and cold air travel through from heating and air conditioning units to the vents on the walls or floors of a home. Over the years the interior lining of the ducts builds up a layer of dirt, dust, and debris that needs to be cleaned out. Clean air ducts provide homeowners with healthier indoor air quality and a more energy-efficient system.

There are two main types of air ducts that can be found in homes. One type is called a flexible duct, which is made of plastic-coated fiberglass. The other type of duct is made of thin sheet metal. Both types are cleaned in essentially the same manner. Either type may be covered on the outside with fiberglass or foil insulation. Be aware that in any home built prior to 1979 there is the possibility of running across asbestos-insulated ducts. Asbestos is a hazardous material that was used to insulate ducts because of its high resistance to heat. When disturbed, asbestos fibers can be released into the air and can be a great danger. Learn how to detect asbestos and do not attempt to clean it under any circumstance.

HOW TO CLEAN AIR DUCTS

1. Make sure that the system is turned off. Begin by cleaning the blower wheel inside of the air conditioning or heating unit with your shop vacuum, being very careful not to damage

the unit or disconnect any wires. In most units the blower wheel will look like a fan. Dirt and oil tend to collect on the blower. If the system has a washable filter, take it outside and clean it with your garden sprayer and make sure that it is dry before you reinstall it. If the filter is not washable, it should be replaced. You can purchase filters at most hardware stores.

2. Ducts usually run in the attic or in the basement. Locate the ducts and disconnect them, starting close to the heating or cooling unit. You will probably need to bring along your droplight because attics and basements tend to be dark. Reach into the duct with the brush attachment on your shop vacuum and gently clean away all dirt on the interior of the duct.

3. Some houses have long and continuous runs of ducts. If they are flexible ducts, cut the duct into sections that you will later reseal with duct tape. If the ducts are metal, you will need to cut access holes in them, which you will later reseal with sheet metal panels that are caulked and secured with sheet metal screws. Continue cleaning the runs of ducts until they are all free of dust and dirt. Then seal them back up.

4. Remove each register and grill from the walls, ceilings, and floors (locations vary from house to house). Reach inside with your shop vacuum and clean as far back as you can reach. Wash off the registers and grills with your garden sprayer and dry them off before you reinstall them.

5. Test out the system by turning it on and checking for dust exiting the vents.

The duct system in an average-size home (3,000 square feet) will take about five hours to clean. Most companies charge from $25 to $40 per register and an additional $50 to $90 to clean the air conditioning and heating unit. Commercial buildings should be estimated per square foot of duct and usually require a crew of several workers to do the job. You will need to go out and estimate these jobs because larger buildings have larger amounts of duct work and it is impossible to give an accurate price over the phone.

ANTIQUE AND COLLECTIBLE DEALING

Start up cost: $0 on up.

Equipment needed: Vehicle with enough space to transport your stock (this is necessary only if you are dealing with large items such as furniture) and antique price guides.

People love to collect antiques for many reasons, such as their beauty, craftsmanship, scarcity, and real and sentimental values. Collectors are willing to pay dearly for the right items. You can get started in your own antique business quite easily, and you don't have to own your own shop to be a successful dealer.

The word *antique* refers to a valuable item that is over 100 years old, although many so-called antiques are not quite that old. Collectibles are items that are not necessarily as old as antiques, but have value to collectors. A good example of collectibles is movie memorabilia from the 1950s.

Start by visiting antique shops, noticing what sort of things are for sale. Ask the shopkeeper questions. You'll find that most shop owners will be happy to chat about their stock. Find out what is hot right now. The needs of the market are constantly changing. Read current antique price guides. There are many available at bookstores. These price guides will give you a good idea of what any particular item is worth and will familiarize you with items to look for.

Most dealers specialize in a particular type of antique or collectible. By being an expert in a few areas of antiques, you will know what is a good deal and what is not. Once you have decided on the type of merchandise you would like to specialize in, go out and start looking. Good places to find antiques are garage and estate sales, thrift shops, flea markets, and auctions. Always keep your price guide handy to make sure that you are getting a good deal. Never buy anything that is not in good shape, such as a chipped plate.

WHERE TO SELL YOUR STOCK

Antique Malls

One of the best ways to sell your collection is to rent a space in an antique mall. An antique mall is an antique shop that rents out display cases or a space inside the shop for a monthly fee. You are in charge of displaying, pricing, and stocking your space. The shopkeeper will show your items for you and handle the sales.

Antique Shops

Antique shops will often take your items on consignment. All you have to do is drop off your items with the shop owner and he or she will sell it for you and take a percentage of the profit (usually about 10 percent).

Private Collectors

If you search through the classified ads in newspapers you will probably find ads from collectors searching for certain items.

RELATED IDEAS

Antique Hunter

If you don't have any money to begin with, you can still get started in antique dealing. Just take out an advertisement in the paper as an antique hunter. An antique hunter is someone who finds antiques for collectors. Collectors will call you and tell you what kind of things they are looking for. You simply go around to antique shops and find what they want and take a photo of the item. Show them the photo, mark up the price of the item (so that you make a profit), and obtain payment. You then go and purchase the item and keep the leftover profit for yourself. Operating as a middleman in this business is usually quite safe if you move quickly. The chances of the item being sold while you wait for your clients to make a decision are quite low because antiques, particularly the more expensive pieces, are not likely to sell quickly.

Auction Driver

Here's a great opportunity if you have a truck or van. At most auctions the auctioneer will ask at the beginning if any-one in the audience is willing to transport merchandise after the show. When a person buys a piece of furniture at an auc-tion, he or she is responsible for moving it off of the property at the end of the day. If you go to the auction with an empty vehicle, you'll likely get a few moving jobs on the spot.

ASPHALT DRIVEWAY SEALING

Start up cost: $300.

Equipment needed: Broom (or air blower), small and large squeegees with long handles, weed trimmer, spatula, crack filler, driveway sealer, hose with sprayer nozzle, and driveway cleaner.

Asphalt driveways deteriorate from weather, grease and oil, and general use. Driveways can be restored and protected, which extends their life and brings them back to their smooth, original condition. Sealing should be done about every five years to protect the surface from moisture, dirt, and chemicals.

FOLLOW THESE STEPS

1. Start off by thoroughly cleaning the driveway. It should be swept free of all dirt and loose debris with a broom or air blower. Hose down the surface and use a grease-cutting driveway cleaner to remove any oily residue. While you are waiting for it to dry off, trim any weeds or grass lining the sides of the driveway. Sweep it one more time to make sure that any loose particles have been removed.

2. Rope off the driveway entrance so that no one drives or walks onto the new sealer you're about to apply.

3. Repair all cracks with a crack filler made for driveways. Follow the manufacturer's instructions and fill the small cracks.

4. Potholes can be repaired with an asphalt patching compound. Remove any loose gravel bits from the hole before filling. Follow the manufacturer's instructions.

5. Starting at the area closest to the garage, pour on the sealer and spread it out with your squeegee, working on a small area at a time and being careful not to let the sealer run off of the sides. Allow the coat to dry and apply a second coat if needed. Follow the manufacturer's directions for best results.

6. Tools and equipment can be cleaned if they are washed immediately after use with soap and water.

AUTO DETAILING

Start up cost: $200.

Equipment needed: See supply list below.

Auto detailing is a fun and profitable business, especially for those who love cars. Many people will get their car detailed when they want it to have that extra attention that most car washes don't provide.

You can detail cars at the customer's home or you could set up shop at a local gas station. Recently, I saw a man who had quite a busy little detailing shop set up in the underground parking garage of a high-rise office building.

HOW TO GET STARTED

1. First, put together a kit with the following items:
   - Car wax
   - Rubbing compound (for scuffs and nicks)
   - Polish designed for auto paint
   - Car soap
   - Scrub brush
   - Sponges
   - Towels
   - Window leaner
   - Chrome polish
   - Leather/vinyl cleaner
   - Rags
   - Vacuum
   - Bucket
   - Chamois
   - Carpet shampoo (for floor mats)
   - Tar remover

- Tire cleaner
- WD-40 (for squeaky doors and sticking antennas)
- High-pressure hose nozzle

2. Read as many books as you can on the subject of car care and auto detailing, educating yourself on how to become a professional in your new business.

3. Detail your own car using the new methods you've learned. Taking before and after photos of your work is a good idea.

4. Decide where you want to operate your business (such as door to door, office building garages, gas stations) and start advertising.

BATHTUB REFINISHING

Start up cost: $300.

Equipment needed: Special tool kit (see list below).

Over the years, bathtubs and sinks can become dull and worn. There are several kits on the market now that make refinishing porcelain surfaces easy and profitable. These kits can be bought at most hardware and tile stores or you can purchase your materials directly from the manufacturer.

HOW TO GET STARTED

1. Besides the refinishing materials, you'll need to put together a kit of the following tools and supplies for your repairs:

- Surface cleaner made with trisodium phosphate (for removing dirt, grease, and soap residue that has become embedded in the porcelain)
- Muriatic acid or a concrete etching product (to thoroughly remove residue)
- Very fine wet-dry sandpaper
- Strong portable fan (for better air circulation)
- Metal buckets (for mixing chemicals)
- Good quality paint brushes with natural bristles
- Paint roller and paint sprayer
- Lacquer thinner and acetone
- Protective clothing, gloves, and respirator

2. Buy the refinishing materials and follow the manufacturer's exact instructions. Do a trial run on an old bathtub

and perfect your skills. Establish your prices, taking your time and materials into consideration.

OTHER IDEAS

- All-purpose tints can be mixed into the enamel to create pastel shades. Sinks and tile can also be refinished.
- Let the local plumbers know about your services—they spend a lot of time in bathrooms—and ask them to refer you to customers with worn tubs.

BEEKEEPING

Start up cost: $300 and up.

Equipment needed: Protective clothing, heavy gloves, movable beehives, and a smoker (a tool used to sedate bees).

Beekeeping can be a fun and profitable business with several moneymaking avenues. Bees make honey that can be sold to consumers. You can also sell beeswax for making candles, soaps, and a multitude of other useful products. Beekeepers commonly rent out their bee hives to farmers to pollinate crops.

HOW TO GET STARTED

1. Before attempting to handle bees, take a class about beekeeping to learn safe bee handling procedures. (Many community colleges offer such classes.) Visiting a local beekeeper would also be a good idea to learn more about the business.

2. Honey and beeswax can be sold through mail order, in shops, at street fairs, and virtually anyplace you find people. Did you know that many people buy locally harvested honey to help with their allergies to the flowers and plants in the area?

3. Bees are generally harmless when handled properly, but check with your city regarding beekeeping ordinances.

BLIND AND SHADE CLEANING

Start up cost: $100.

Equipment needed: Vacuum, blind cleaning brush called a Tricket (available at hardware stores), mild detergent, drop cloth, standard tool kit, and towels.

Many homes and businesses now have blinds or shades in place of the traditional drapery. Although regular dusting and cleaning of metal blinds and shades is usually effective, there are times when professional cleaning is needed. Blind cleaning is simple and easy.

HOW TO CLEAN BLINDS

1. Begin cleaning by opening up the blinds and thoroughly dusting both sides of the metal slats using a Tricket. Then vacuum using an upholstery brush.
2. Unscrew the head box (the long, square box at the top of the blinds) from the wall and take the blinds outside. Lay the blinds out flat on a drop cloth.
3. Scrub both sides of the slats with a soft-bristled scrub brush or sponge using a mild detergent. (Dish washing liquid mixed with warm water will work.)
4. Hang the blinds up over a wall or clothesline and rinse with a hose until all of the soap solution is rinsed off.
5. Towel dry the blinds and rehang.

OTHER IDEAS

- Water should not be used to clean wooden blinds. Use furniture polish or mineral spirits instead. Apply the cleaner and wipe immediately using a blind cleaning brush.
- Broken blinds and shades can be repaired, which is a useful skill to learn in this business.

BOAT BOTTOM CLEANING

Start up cost: $300.

Equipment needed: Diving or snorkel gear, boat cleaning products, and cleaning brushes.

Boat bottom cleaning? Believe it or not, this can be a lucrative business and lots of fun if you enjoy being in the water. The following is the true story of a highly paid executive who was laid off from his job at a large corporation and turned his dreams into a gold mine.

After being laid off from his job, Bill decided to go down to his boat and spend a little time there reorganizing his life. He'd always loved sailing and diving, so this was the perfect place to retreat. He began cleaning his boat, which had been neglected and was basically just sitting there in the dock except for the occasional weekend trip. Soon enough, he got the boat back in tip-top shape, all except for the bottom, which had accumulated a layer of crud on it. Being little tight on cash, Bill couldn't afford the $500 bottom-cleaning fee, which involved lifting the boat out of the water to clean its underside. Looking for any excuse to put on his diving gear, he solved the boat scum problem by diving under his boat and cleaning it himself with a cleaning product and scrub brushes. He discovered that he could do just as good a job as the cleaning service.

When Bill came up after cleaning, he saw his curious neighbor, whose boat was docked next to his. The neighbor asked, "What are you doing down there?" Bill told the man and offered to clean his boat for half the fee the other cleaning service would have charged. That's how it all began.

Word got out around the dock about Bill and his boat bottom cleaning. Other boat owners began hiring him. Bill rode around in a small motor boat and cleaned almost every boat in the marina, saving people money and making himself a bundle. Every time he was under water he'd take a quick look at the boat in the next slip and if it was dirty, he'd leave one of his business cards, letting them know that it was time for a cleaning. If you live near the ocean or a lake, you can start your own service just like Bill did.

HOW TO GET STARTED

1. Go to a boat supply store and find out about the cleaning products available.

2. Advertise by leaving fliers or business cards on the boats.

3. Once you're established, build up a list of clients that you can send reminders to every year for a recleaning.

OTHER IDEAS

- As well as cleaning boat bottoms, you could start a service that cleans the whole boat. Boat cleaning is hard work and many owners would be happy to pay someone else to do it.

CARPET CLEANING

Start up cost: $600.

Equipment needed: Carpet steam cleaner, powerful vacuum, carpet shampoo (compatible with steam cleaner), foam or powdered carpet cleaner (for removing spots and stains), towels, nylon scrub brush, and broom. (These supplies can be purchased from a janitorial supply house.)

In the lifetime of every carpet there comes a point when regular vacuuming and routine maintenance are not enough. Professional steam cleaning is needed every few years to remove embedded soil and tough stains. Steam cleaning will help restore the carpet back to its original beauty. The following method can be used to clean both wool and synthetic carpets.

HOW TO CLEAN CARPETS

1. Begin by giving the carpet a thorough vacuuming. This will help to remove loose dirt and particles from the surface.

2. Clean all spots and stains on the carpet. This can be done by using a foam or powdered carpet cleaner. Follow the manufacturer's instructions. You may find that some tougher stains need to be scrubbed out. Use your nylon scrub brush to break up the stain. Blot it out using a damp towel.

3. To use the steam cleaner, fill the tank with hot water and compatible cleaning solution following the manufacturer's instructions. Starting in the corner of the room, turn on the machine and hold the dispensing nozzle close to the floor. Squeeze the solution release trigger so that the carpet's surface is covered (but not soaked) and pull the wand along toward you about 4 feet. Release the trigger and work the solution

into the carpet by pushing it back and forth over the area. Repeat the process on the next section of carpet until the entire surface has been cleaned. When cleaning is done with the steamer, brush the carpet's damp surface with a broom to prevent flattening. Note that heavily soiled "traffic" areas may need to be cleaned a second time.

OTHER IDEAS

- There are solutions available that waterproof carpet and upholstery and that can be applied after cleaning to extend the life of the carpet. Offer to apply it for an additional charge. Check with a janitorial supply house to find these products.

CASH IN ON YOUR TALENTS

Start up cost: Varies.

Equipment needed: Varies.

Do you have a special talent that you can teach to others? Thousands of individuals are cashing in on their abilities by teaching classes or private lessons.

CONSIDER THESE IDEAS

- Musical instruments
- Singing
- Acting
- Art
- Computer instruction
- Self-defense
- Cooking
- Dance
- Exercise
- Foreign languages
- Swimming
- Tennis
- Tutoring
- Typing
- Sewing

HOW TO GET STARTED

1. Decide what kind of class or lessons you would like to teach and figure out how to teach it to beginners, starting at an easy level.

2. Advertise your class or lessons. If you want to teach group lessons you'll need to advertise a few weeks in advance. (For group lessons, reserve a site with adequate space.)

TIP

- Some schools would be happy to have you teach an extension class. Call up your local school district to find out how to go about it.

CATERING HIGH-RISE OFFICE BUILDINGS

Start up cost: $100.

Equipment needed: Large cooler, Styrofoam or plastic food containers, plastic cutlery, single-use condiment packs, napkins, and a small furniture dolly (optional).

This is a great business if you love to prepare food and live in a big city or area with high-rise office buildings. Most people working in these buildings are often too busy to go out for a decent meal and get tired of eating the same old bagged lunches or take-out burgers day after day. Offering a fresh and healthy variety of foods to office workers is a welcome and profitable service.

HOW TO GET STARTED

1. Decide what kind of foods you want to offer with your catering service. Fresh sandwiches, muffins, brownies, bagels with cream cheese, cake, vegetable sticks (like carrots and celery), and salads are popular items. Buy single-use packs of mayonnaise, mustard, and salad dressings and have them on hand. You may also want to experiment with your own special dishes like enchiladas, chili, or lasagna, all of which can be microwaved.

2. Buy your cooler and supplies (see above) from a restaurant supplier.

3. Prepare and package your food. It is important that your items be attractive and wrapped or boxed in such a way that the quality and freshness is preserved.

4. Pack up your cooler with ice and food just before you leave your kitchen. Take the food to a large office building about twenty minutes before lunchtime and work your way up to the top floor. Tell the receptionist that you have lunch available for anyone interested. Those first few visits may be a little awkward, but after you've been there a few times, you'll soon find employees anticipating your arrival and you'll have a good idea of how much food you'll need to bring along on your route and what items are the best sellers.

TIPS

- Survey your clients by asking if there is some particular item that they would like added to your menu.
- Carry a small amount of cash (enough to make change for your customers).
- Find out if you are required to carry a special permit for food preparation in your area.
- It might be necessary to first get permission from the managers of the buildings that you will be working in.

OTHER IDEAS

- Having a second cooler available with ice-cold sodas and bottled juices will bring you additional sales.

CEILING AND WALL CLEANING

Start up cost: $300.

Equipment needed: Lambswool duster with extension attachment, "Dry Sponge" with extension attachment, buckets, ladder, regular sponges, bleach cleaner, garden sprayer, plastic tarps, white shoe polish, cloths, and degreasing cleaning solution.

Ceilings and walls need to be cleaned every few years to remove dirt, grease, smoke, and spots. Although these high surfaces don't take the same abuse as floors, they still need proper care. There are several types of ceilings and just as many methods to clean them.

HOW TO CLEAN CEILINGS AND WALLS

For all types of ceilings and walls, begin by removing loose dirt with a lambswool duster. You can either use a ladder to reach the surface or purchase extension poles. Wipe the surface in long strokes. Shake the duster outside every few minutes to clean it and to avoid releasing dust back into the house.

Latex Painted Ceilings

For surfaces coated with latex paint, a regular cleaning should do the job. Mix up a solution of surface cleaner and water in a bucket. Dip a sponge into the solution, then scrub gently until the dirt is removed from the surface. When the sponge starts to get dirty, rinse it out in a clean bucket of water. Dip the sponge in the cleaning solution again and continue. Wipe away any excess water with a towel. You can use a ladder and reach up by hand or you can attach your sponge to an extension pole. In some cases, a regular kitchen mop with a soft sponge on the end will work well.

Matte-Finished Surfaces

These surfaces need extra care and cannot be cleaned with a water-based solution. You will need to use a dry sponge, which is specifically designed to clean such surfaces without the use of water. Wipe the sponge across the surface in even strokes. When the sponge begins to blacken, turn it over and use the other side. When the sponge is dirty on both sides, throw it out. It cannot be washed and can only be used one time.

"Cottage Cheese" Ceilings and Acoustical Tiles

These types of ceilings tend to collect more dirt than any other due to their porous nature. In some cases a dry sponge will do the job. It may be necessary, though, to clean the surface with a bleach solution. There is a special bleach for ceilings that can be purchased from a janitorial supplier. This type of cleaning will get rid of any yellowing and stains. In most cases the solution can be applied with a garden sprayer. Follow the manufacturer's instructions. For this type of cleaning you will need to lay down plastic tarps while working to avoid damaging other items in the home.

TIPS

- Kitchen ceilings and walls may have accumulated a layer of dirty grease. In some cases a degreasing solution can be applied to remove the build up.
- Spots and stains that did not come off during the regular cleaning process can be camouflaged with a matching paint or with white shoe polish.

CHANDELIER CLEANING

Start up cost: $300.

Equipment needed: Tall step ladder, vacuum cleaner with soft brush attachments, instant camera, drop cloths, plastic buckets, spray bottles, cotton rags, chandelier cleaning solution, ammonia, plastic bags, standard tool box and tools, needle-nose pliers, roll of thin wire (for rehanging crystals if necessary).

Brilliant chandeliers are the focal point of many rooms and lobbies. Over the years, crystal chandeliers can look less than dazzling after accumulating layers of dust and grease that dull their sparkle. These sparkling beauties can be restored to their original brilliance with a good cleaning. You'll find chandeliers in many homes, hotels, and buildings. Chandelier cleaning is a great business because many homeowners and building maintenance people find them hard to reach and either don't know how or don't want to take the time to clean them.

HOW TO GET STARTED

1. Place a large tarp on the floor beneath the chandelier. Place additional towels or tarps on top of the tarp to soak up any solution that may drip during the cleaning.

2. Standing on a ladder, use a shop vacuum to remove any dust and debris from the chandelier. For large chandeliers that hang high, you may need to rent a platform lift.

3. Tape off any metal hardware with masking tape and cover the bulbs with plastic bags.

4. Fill a large spray bottle with chandelier cleaning solution and spray it onto the crystals. Let the chandelier drip dry.

5. Remove the plastic and masking tape.

TIPS

- It's a good idea to take a photo of the chandelier before cleaning in case any of the crystals are knocked off. This will help you to replace them in the right place.
- Some chandeliers may need more than a spray cleaning. You'll have to do this by hand. The best way is to remove the crystals and polish them with a soft cloth dipped in your cleaning solution.

CHILD-PROOFING
HOMES

Start up cost: None.

Equipment needed: None.

AN OUNCE OF PREVENTION
IS WORTH A POUND OF CURE

Prevention is the name of the game when it comes to child-proofing a house. You can provide an invaluable service to the parents in your community by offering a service that helps them keep their children safe indoors and outdoors. All you'll need is a keen eye for spotting and handling potentially hazardous scenarios.

HOW TO GET STARTED

1. Get educated. The library is a great place to start and has many reference books on child safety. You can also write to the following organizations for more information:

- National Safety Council
  444 N. Michigan Avenue
  Chicago, IL 60611
- National SAFE KIDS Campaign
  111 Michigan Avenue N.W.
  Washington, DC 20010
- You should also get information from your local poison center.

2. Make up a checklist of all the points to check in a home (poisons, firearms, sharp objects and corners, lists of

emergency phone numbers, medicines, cabinet locks, swimming pool, electrical outlets, working smoke alarms, gate and guards, and so forth).

3. Go into homes with your checklist to spot and handle all points of danger. There are many child-proofing items available on the market that you may need to purchase for a particular job, such as outlet covers, corner guards, and fencing. You should charge each customer for an inspection and any safety accessories that they will need to make their home child-proof.

IMPORTANT NOTE

• Remember, your clients are depending on you to find and correct potential hazards in their homes. This is a responsibility that cannot be taken lightly. Check with an attorney to find out if any special licenses or contracts are required for your business.

CHIMNEY SWEEPING

Start up cost: $600.

Equipment needed: Extension ladder, vehicle (equipped to carry ladder and materials), chimney sweeping brushes with extension poles, shop vacuum, droplight, extension cord, tarps, masking tape, heavy work gloves, respirator, goggles, and standard tool kit.

Despite what the fairy tales may have implied, chimney sweeping is hard and dirty work. Nevertheless, this type of business consistently proves to be lucrative. With growing homeowner awareness of chimney fires and with a bit of simple promotion like passing out flyers to local residents, it's often difficult to keep up with the consumer demand for this service (especially in the fall and winter seasons).

Chimneys need to be inspected and in most cases cleaned once a year. Hazardous layers of creosote or "soot" build up in the interior of the chimney with every fire that is burned. Creosote is a highly flammable substance that must be swept out of the chimney to prevent chimney fires and, in many cases, to reestablish draft efficiency. Chimneys can also be foul smelling if they are not regularly cleaned.

HOW TO CLEAN CHIMNEYS

1. Inspect the chimney first from the fireplace by shining a droplight down from the roof. Also examine the firebox to make sure that there is no structural damage such as missing bricks, large cracks, or even apparently minor interior cracks. (Even minor interior cracks can be very dangerous.) Have the homeowner contact a licensed contractor or mason experienced in chimney work if such a situation is found and

instruct the homeowner to not use his or her fireplace or chimney-related heating system until it is fixed.

If it looks okay, proceed with the cleaning. If there are small cracks or loose bricks (either or both being in the firebox) you can repair them by patching with 20 percent fireclay mixed with 80 percent mortar.

2. Most fireplaces have a damper. Open it (usually by pulling the handle toward you). Look up from the bottom to make sure it is open. Seal off the fireplace completely from inside the home using a heavy tarp and high-quality masking tape. The tarp will prevent soot from entering the home while you are cleaning.

3. From the roof, sweep downward with a wire chimney sweeping brush using long strokes. The brush should be the size of the flue (the opening going up the inside of the chimney and extending to the top so the smoke can escape) or slightly larger. By using extension poles you should be able to brush the length of the chimney.

4. Open up the tarp at the bottom just enough to insert the shop vacuum nozzle so that soot can be sucked up without soiling the home. Carefully remove the tarp from the fireplace and clean out the firebox by pushing the ashes into the ash pit. Vacuum out the remaining ashes and soot with your shop vacuum. Be sure to clean the interior shelf above the damper. Clean the walls that the brush did not reach. A chimney gets wider at the bottom and almost always must be cleaned from the bottom as well. Use small wire brushes and small dust brushes for the bottom part.

Always have the vacuum running while you are cleaning the bottom of the chimney, and have the nozzle in the firebox to immediately suck up the dust. Some sweeps like to have the nozzle running while cleaning the top as well. In this case, the nozzle is inserted carefully in the firebox, along the floor, with a very good seal (from the tarp) around the hose. The whole firebox is still sealed off with the same tarp.

OTHER IDEAS

- If the chimney has no covering at the top, you should install a spark arrestor or a chimney cap. A spark arrestor is a wire mesh screen that fits over the top of the chimney to prevent sparks and burning embers from escaping. It can be purchased from a chimney sweep supplier. A chimney cap is a heavy-duty cover that fits on top of the chimney. It lets the smoke escape through its metal mesh sides and keeps out water and nesting birds with its solid metal top. Chimney caps are a great accessory to sell to your customers and are far better than just a spark arrestor.
- Wearing the traditional uniform of a chimney sweep (a black top hat and tails) will add charm and a touch of class to your business. Many people believe that shaking hands with a chimney sweep is good luck and will be happy to have you work in their home.

ADDITIONAL ACCESSORIES THAT CAN BE SOLD

- Heat shields. Heat shields are metal panels that are installed at the rear wall of the fire box to help reflect more heat into the home.
- Smoke guards. Smoke guards are installed on the outside of the firebox and help to deter smoke from entering the home.
- Fireplace tools (pokers, shovels, and tongs).

COSTUMED
TELEGRAMS

Start up cost: $100 on up.

Equipment needed: Costumes.

Imagine the surprise if a giant chicken delivered a birthday present to your door or if someone wearing a gorilla costume came to your office to congratulate a coworker on a promotion! You can start your own unique telegram service with little money. All you'll need is a few wild and zany costumes. Besides delivering messages and gifts, you'll also be delivering something that money can't buy: Smiles.

HOW TO GET STARTED

1. Advertise your services in the local phone book under "Telegrams" and make up a few flyers that can be mailed or delivered to offices and homes in your city.

2. Choose your costumes. If you can't afford to buy them, but are handy with a sewing machine, you can make your own. Fabric stores have special costume patterns available. Another option is to rent your costumes. If you choose to rent, make sure that the particular costume you need will be available.

3. Offer to deliver gifts, messages, and food.

TIPS

- Contact local shops that sell flowers and gifts. Let them know that you'll deliver for them in costume.
- Since you'll have costumes on hand with your new business, use them to entertain at children's parties on the weekends.

CURB PAINTING SERVICE

Start up cost: $50.

Equipment needed: Paint, masking tape, and numerical stencils.

It can be frustrating when the numbers painted on a curb in front of a home can't be read or seen. Weather conditions and infrequent repainting cause them to fade away over the years. Since most cities don't maintain curb numbers, a curb painting service can be a profitable and needed business. This type of work is quick and easy to sell to homeowners.

HOW TO GET STARTED

Put together a painting kit including the following items:

- White exterior paint (quick drying type)
- Black spray paint
- Numerical stencil set (3-inch size)
- Masking tape
- Several wide paint brushes
- Scrub brush
- Spray bottle
- Ruler

Knock on doors in your neighborhood and introduce yourself as a curb number painter. Tell your potential customer that you'll be working in the neighborhood today and would like to repaint the numbers on their curb. When they agree to have you do the work, collect the money and start painting.

FOLLOW THESE EASY STEPS

1. Spray the portion of the curb with water and scrub off any dirt or oil on the surface.

2. When the surface is dry, paint over the old, faded paint job with a wide paint brush and white exterior paint and let it dry.

3. Using masking tape and a ruler, align the numerical stencils over the white area and fill in the numbers with black spray paint.

With a little practice, you'll find that you can do a job in just minutes. Move on to the next home and repeat the steps above.

OTHER IDEAS

- You may want to offer the additional service of installing metal or decorative ceramic tile numbers on the customer's house to increase address visibility. These numbers are available at hardware stores.

DOG OBEDIENCE TRAINING

Start up cost: $100.

Equipment needed: None.

If you love dogs, this could be a fun and profitable part-time business for you. Most dogs need some form of guidance and training, as many a frustrated owner knows.

HOW TO GET STARTED

1. If you don't know how to train a dog, you can learn quite easily. There are many books and videos on the subject. Do some research and try out the different methods on your own dog until you find one that you're happy and comfortable with.

2. Once you've got your own dog in tip-top shape, try out your training method on a friend or neighbor's dog to ensure that your skills are good enough to teach a class.

3. When you're confident and ready to go, you should begin by picking out a location. You can get permission to use a local park or you can rent a large room at a community center. Make sure that your location has plenty of space and be sure to reserve it for the times you'll be holding the class.

4. Decide what sort of fee to charge for your class and take out an ad in the classifieds several weeks in advance.

Posting notices on bulletin boards and in neighborhood pet shops could also be helpful.

OTHER IDEAS

- Private lessons can be given at the dog owner's home for a higher fee.

DOORBELL REPAIR/ REPLACEMENT

Start up cost: $100.

Equipment needed: Standard tool kit, circuit tester, wire cutters/strippers, fine sand paper, supply of wire, spare doorbell parts, silicone spray, and cleaning cloths.

Quite often you will find that the doorbell on a home does not chime when the button is pushed. This is a common problem and the average homeowner has no idea how to remedy it. Many people let this problem persist for years. Doorbell repair and replacement is an easy job that can become an easy and profitable business. The supplies that you will need (see above) can be purchased at a hardware store or from an electronics supplier.

HOW TO REPAIR A DOORBELL

1. Push the button to test it. If it does not chime, remove the push button mounting from the outside wall by unscrewing it or by prying it off with a screwdriver.
2. With your circuit tester, test the current by touching it to the place on the button where the wires are connected. If the bulb lights up, too much current is flowing through the system and indicates a faulty transformer (see step 6). If the bulb does not light, continue with this step. Using fine grade sand paper, sand the ends of the loose wires until they are shiny and bright or clip off the old ends and strip away $\frac{1}{2}$ inch of the plastic coating exposing the new ends. Reconnect the wires back on the push button by bending them around the screws and try the bell again. If it works, reinstall the

push button mounting. If it does not work, continue on to step 3.

3. Unscrew the wires again and test them by touching both wire ends together with a screw driver. If there is a spark or the bell rings, reconnect the wires tightly. If there is no spark, you'll need to replace the push button.

4. If there is no spark and the bell doesn't work, disconnect the push button wires and twist them together. Disconnect one of the wires that is connected to the bell or chimes. Touch the disconnected bell wire to the connected bell wire. If it sparks, the bell connection is working, but something is wrong with the bell or transformer. Continue to the next step.

5. The bell or chime is activated by a small current that is activated when the push button is depressed. The current causes a plunger to strike a metal bar or bars, which produces a tone. Sometimes the plungers get dirty and become sluggish or stop working. Remove the chime unit and clean its parts with a cloth. Make sure that no parts are missing. Using silicone spray, lubricate the chimes and bars.

6. Test the bell wires again. If you don't get a spark, you'll need to check the transformer. It is the device that reduces the regular household current from 115–120 volts down to less than 16 volts, which is all that is necessary to operate a doorbell. Follow the push button wires to the transformer—a metal rectangular device about 3×2 inches. Check the circuit breaker or fuse on the household circuit to which it is attached. Reset the breaker or fuse if needed. Test the transformer by touching the circuit tester to the part of the transformer where the thin wires are attached. If the transformer is working, your circuit tester should light up. If the transformer does not seem to be working, disconnect its power and clean and tighten its wiring. Test it again and if it still doesn't work, replace it. With the new transformer,

test the bell again. If it still doesn't get a spark, the bell will need to be replaced or repaired.

IMPORTANT NOTE

- Before you attempt to repair a doorbell, you must learn about basic electricity and doorbell repair. You can find information on both subjects in household repair guides.

DRYER DUCT CLEANING

Start up cost: $400.

Equipment needed: Truck or vehicle (equipped to carry a ladder), extension ladder, shop vacuum, duct tape, basic tool kit, and a 4-inch chimney-sweeping brush with flexible extension poles.

Did you know that when a dryer exhaust duct gets clogged with lint it might take up to four hours to dry a single load of clothes? When a dryer duct gets stopped up it dramatically reduces the efficiency of the appliance and can become a dangerous fire hazard. According to the Consumer Product Safety Commission, 13,900 clothes dryer fires occurred in the United States in 1987, resulting in 20 deaths, 180 injuries, and property loss estimated at more than $40 million. In most of these cases, according to the National Fire Protection Association, the culprit was lint.

Most people don't think about cleaning the dryer duct. It's usually not until after they call their dryer repairman out because their clothes aren't drying that they discover the real problem is within the duct. Most of the repair companies don't clean the ducts and this is where you and your cleaning company can step in.

The going rate for cleaning ranges between $50 and $100 and the average job takes a little less than an hour. One company charges a $45 service call plus $45 an hour. Most of their customers call them back every year or two for a repeat cleaning.

There are two types of dryers—those that run on gas and those that run on electricity. The venting for both types is the same. The exhaust duct is the tubing that runs from the dryer and out the side of the wall or to the roof. There are two types of ducts, one made of a flexible plastic material (called "flex duct") and one made of rigid aluminum piping. Both types are generally about 4 inches in diameter and vary in length depending on their routing. The most common length is from 4 to 20 feet.

Every time a load of clothes is dried, hot air is pushed into the dryer drum and forced out through the lint trap. The trap, which is a screen, catches most of the lint, but not all of it. The lint then travels through the exhaust duct and gradually builds up within the interior lining, catching on the grooves and kinks of the duct. Eventually the buildup causes an air blockage. When the exhaust duct is blocked, the dryer will overheat, turn itself off completely, or blow only cool air into the drum and stop drying the clothing inside.

HOW TO CLEAN A DRYER DUCT

The easiest and best way to clean a dryer duct is by manual sweeping. This is done by disconnecting the 4-inch duct from the back of the dryer (or side depending on the model) and running a small chimney sweeping brush all the way through it to where it vents to outside. The rough bristles on the brush will force out the lint clog, which can usually be pulled out by hand or with your shop vacuum.

Each home and each duct routing is different, so you might come across some tough cases such as an apartment building with a duct that vents out the side wall three stories up. In a case like this, you might have to get out your extension ladder and sweep downward from the outside of the building and pull out the clog from the opposite end. Every so often, you might find yourself removing a bird's nest or bee hive from a duct. I would suggest starting on houses and working your way up to the more difficult jobs after you've gained some experience.

Before you begin cleaning dryer ducts, familiarize yourself with the different models and types of dryers. You can buy service manuals from your local appliance dealer or directly from the manufacturer. They will come in handy. Another good way to learn about the business is by purchasing an inexpensive dryer duct repair kit from one of the better-stocked hardware stores. The kit will include a full set of instructions and all of the materials you'll need to fix an old or damaged duct.

Once you're all set up and ready to start, give your local appliance repair shops and plumbers a call to tell them about your services. They will probably be your best source of referrals because they run across clogged dryer ducts on a daily basis.

TIP

- Besides studying the manufacturers' manuals, you should also read books about dryer and appliance repair, which are available in most libraries.

OTHER IDEAS

Replacing Ducts

Once you are familiar with the business, you might want to get into replacing old, worn out ducts. The preferred ducting (aluminum or aluminum flex duct) is very inexpensive and can be bought through an air conditioning supply house or at larger hardware stores.

A 1987 service memo from the Whirlpool Corporation says, "Do not use non-metal flexible duct since it is a potential fire hazard. Non-metal duct will kink, cause lint buildup within the exhaust system, reduce airflow, and create service problems for the dryer." In 1984, Underwriters Laboratory, an independent testing agency that helps set safety standards, recommended also "that only rigid or flexible metal duct should be used to vent dryers." Plastic or vinyl accordion type ducting should be avoided.

FIREWOOD SERVICE

Start up cost: $300.

Equipment needed: Chain saw, ax, extension ladder, and vehicle (equipped to carry ladder and wood).

There's nothing nicer than a roaring fire in the fireplace. Whether for warmth or aesthetics, there will always be a demand for a firewood service that provides precut logs to its customers in small or large amounts.

HOW TO GET STARTED

1. If you don't have your own wooded lot, contact your local office of the Forest Service. Many county and national parks issue permits to firewood services to cut in heavily wooded areas and to remove dead or fallen trees. Find out what their guidelines are; they vary from park to park. You will need a permit to cut trees if you do not own the property.

2. After you have obtained a permit, you can begin cutting trees specified by the park. Cut the trees into small pieces (about 2 feet long) that will fit nicely into a fireplace.

3. Haul the wood and store it in the sunlight so that it can dry out. Different types of wood will take varying amounts of drying time. If you live in an area where there is frequent rain or snow, store the wood in an enclosed area such as a garage or shed to keep it dry.

4. Wrap your wood into small bundles (six or seven pieces) by using a heavy-duty cellophane wrap. These small bundles can be sold to markets or to individual households.

You can also sell the wood in larger amounts such as a cord or a half-cord that will keep a customer stocked up for the entire season.

TIP

- You can also sell bundles of kindling, which are small, thin pieces of wood that help to get the fire started. Split a few of your regular logs into four or five pieces with your ax.

GIFT BASKETS

Start up cost: $200–$1,000.

Equipment needed: Baskets, filler, cellophane, packing tape, ribbons, and stock.

Gift baskets have become very popular gifts over the past few years. From corporate presents to baby showers, holidays, and birthdays, gift baskets are the perfect gift because they can be tailored to suit the tastes of anyone. A woman in Los Angeles started a gift basket business out of her garage and in just a few years has expanded the operation to a giant assembly line warehouse. She also has her own gift basket boutique in a very upscale neighborhood. Being in Los Angeles, she began promoting her gift basket business to the local movie studios. Her persistent efforts soon paid off. One of the major studios now hires her company every year to make thousands of holiday gift baskets for its employees and associates. That one account alone makes her enough profit to live very comfortably.

Gift baskets are very versatile. They can be filled with chocolates, teas, coffee, candy, bath products, toys, or baby things. The possibilities are only limited by your imagination.

HOW TO GET STARTED

1. Buy a small quantity of each item from the equipment needed listed above and make up some beautiful sample baskets. The way you display items inside the basket is very important in this business, so practice with different packaging styles until you're satisfied with the end result. Make several different types of baskets and give each a theme, such as "Honeymooners," which would be a basket

for newlyweds complete with a bottle of champagne and some treats, or "Chocolate Lovers," which would be an assortment of chocolate products.

2. Take photos of your baskets and make up a brochure listing the contents of each basket and its price. Pricing should be based on at least a 50 percent markup of your material cost or more if the market can bear it.

3. Send your brochures to large companies. You can also sell your baskets through mail order and in local shops.

TIPS

- The materials for making gift baskets can be found at craft stores and import shops.
- By offering local delivery, you can increase your business.
- Some other themes for gift baskets could be "Get Well Soon," which would have a pretty bowl and some packets of instant chicken soup; "Bon Voyage," which would have travel-size toiletries; "Suds," which would have an assortment of bubble baths and soaps; and "Wine Lovers," which would have an assortment of miniature wine bottles, cheese, and crackers.

GRAFFITI CLEANUP

Start up cost: $200.

Equipment needed: Ladder, sandpaper, painting supplies (brushes, rollers, trays, bucket, and paint).

Unfortunately, graffiti is an ugly problem in many cities. A graffiti removal service is a welcome business in communities plagued with this problem.

Recently, a group of citizens and business owners in Los Angeles got together to solve the graffiti problem in their neighborhood. They had discovered that gang members and "taggers" used graffiti to communicate with each other. By erasing their ugly messages from the walls, the gangs became frustrated and moved on, ceasing to destroy property in that particular neighborhood.

Solicit businesses and homeowners who have graffiti on their property. You may be hired to do the job on the spot.

HOW TO CLEAN GRAFFITI

Start the job by washing the wall or affected area with water and a mild detergent. When the surface is dry, do a test patch with paint to ensure that the color matches. Remember that paint sometimes dries darker or lighter, so wait for it to dry before you begin. Paint over the graffiti and take special care to see that the new coat blends in with the original. Graffiti can sometimes be removed from concrete by using rough sandpaper.

When the job is satisfactorily completed and you've been paid, leave a business card with the customer for future use. You should also drop off some cards with the residents and neighbors in the area. Chances are that they also have the same problem with vandals.

OTHER IDEAS

- Check with your local hardware store or paint supplier for products that can be applied over your paint job to create a slick surface. If the vandals come back, the protective coating will help repel their spray paint and make cleanup easier.
- Visit a janitorial supply company for special solvents and cleaners to remove graffiti from surfaces such as wood, plastic, and other unpainted surfaces.

GREETING CARDS

Start up cost: $0.

Equipment needed: An imagination.

Have you ever found yourself browsing through the greeting card racks and thinking, "I could write something like that!" Guess what? You can join the thousands of freelance greeting card writers.

The greeting card business is bigger than ever and always looking for bright new slogans, sentimental passages, and outrageous gag lines. In fact, most of the independent card companies buy their ideas from unknown writers.

Fifty percent of all first-class mail consists of greeting cards. Card companies depend on writers to supply them with new ideas and special words to keep up with the consumer demand.

HOW TO GET STARTED

1. Familiarize yourself with the different types of greeting cards available by browsing through the racks at the stores.

2. Ask the clerk which type or line is the best seller.

3. Once you've found a line of cards that you like, take a look at the company name on the back. Send them a note requesting their submission guidelines or catalog. Be sure to include a SASE with your letter.

You will find that submission procedures vary from company to company. Some may request a batch of five to fifteen ideas at a time while others may require you to first sign a disclosure contract that ensures that your ideas and material are original and have not been sent out to other companies.

You'll also find that payment for card ideas varies anywhere from $10 to $100 per card. Most of the companies will buy on a per card basis, although you may find a few who pay royalties.

TIP

- You can find the names and addresses of greeting card publishers in the reference section at the library.

HAULING SERVICE

Start up cost: $400.

Equipment needed: Truck or trailer to haul large items, furniture dolly, heavy work gloves, basic tool kit, ropes and bungee cords (for securing items while hauling), tarps, work light, and trash bags.

Most people have something in their yard, garage, or attic that they'd like to have hauled away. The trash services usually won't pick up tree branches, old sofas, and other large items. You can step in and provide a very needed hauling service.

HOW TO GET STARTED

1. You'll need to have a truck or trailer that is large enough to transport items. If you can't afford to buy one now, rent one and add it into your fee.
2. Find out where the landfills are located in your area and what their rules and regulations are regarding various trash items. They might not accept things like old cans of paint or used motor oil. Also, call local thrift shops and find out what kinds of items they accept. If you haul away an item for a customer, make sure that you have a place to take it, otherwise you'll be stuck with it.
3. Advertise your services to homeowners, real estate agents, property managers, and anyone who might have a need for cleaning up a piece of property.

OTHER IDEAS

- Some of the "junk" that you're hired to haul away might have some value to it. Keep an eye out for items that can be resold, like old furniture, lumber, appliances, and such.
- Advertise your services by offering a "Spring Cleaning Special" or attic/garage clean up.

HOME CARE FOR THE ELDERLY OR SICK

Start up cost: $0.

Equipment needed: None.

Home care for elderly and sick persons is a rapidly growing business with today's skyrocketing costs of nursing homes and live-in nurses. Many elderly and sick people or their families need someone that can stop by daily and help out. Your clients could range from an elderly man who needs help cooking to a new mother who is recovering from a difficult birth and needs help caring for her baby. You could provide such services as cooking hot meals, light cleaning, vacuuming, dusting, help with personal grooming, transportation and escorts to the market and library, or any number of other tasks that may be needed.

Make it clear to your clients that you will not be providing any sort of medical care for them. Your business consists of strictly household and personal service. Although you aren't required to have formal training and a license or certification, the National Home Caring Council recommends that home aides have sixty hours of training in personal care, home safety, and basic nursing. Such training is available through community college programs. If you enjoy bringing cheer and smiles to those around you, this could be a good business for you to start.

Advertise your services by leaving cards or flyers at a local community center for the elderly. You might also try contacting nursing homes, doctors, and hospitals and get their permission to leave a few cards with them. (See the chapter in this book on advertising.) Make sure you have a list of references available that your potential clients can call.

Friends, relatives, and current clients who are pleased with your services are your best references.

ONCE YOU HAVE A CLIENT OR CLIENTS

1. Make up a schedule with each client and specify what days and at what time you will be coming over.

2. Draw up a list of the services that are needed on what days.

3. Put together a list of emergency phone numbers. This should include your client's doctor, family members, friends, hospital, and so on. Keep the list handy in case you need it in an emergency.

TIPS

- Be patient with elderly and sick people as they may sometimes be irritable or grumpy. Kindness and understanding will help you get through those frustrating moments.
- Do whatever you can to make your clients more comfortable and happy. This could be as simple as saying a few kind words or bringing some extra pillows.

HOMEMADE TREATS

Start up cost: $200.

Equipment needed: Baking equipment, ingredients, cellophane wrap, and labels.

Homemade dessert items are big sellers. You can walk into almost any convenience store and find a vast array of homemade brownies, cookies, fudge, carrot cake, and other delightful confections. You can sell your goods to stores for ten times the cost of your materials and make a nice profit.

HOW TO GET STARTED

1. Bake or make up several batches of your homemade goods. Wrap them in thick, clear cellophane secured with a decorative label that tells the consumer what it is, the ingredients used, and your company name and address.

2. Take samples of your creations to local convenience stores, gas stations, liquor stores, restaurants, and anyplace else snacks are sold and leave them with the owner or manager to try. If you can't get an order on the spot, get a business card and follow up the next day with a phone call. Continue on to the next store until you've made some sales.

3. When you make a sale, establish a delivery route with your customer, offering to replace old or unsold stock. Make sure that your prices are high enough for you to make a profit and for the store to also make a profit after their mark-up.

TIPS

- Check with your city about food preparation laws.
- Offer a unique product. A friend of mine specializes in sugar-free cookies and muffins and sells her freshly baked goods to local health food stores.

HOUSE CLEANING

Start up cost: $200.

Equipment needed: Basic cleaning kit (see list below) and a vehicle if you plan to travel.

House cleaning is a big business these days. In the average American family, both mom and dad are holding jobs in order to make ends meet, which leaves little time for cleaning the house. In more affluent neighborhoods, many people enjoy the luxury of not having to do the cleaning. Scrubbing floors and dusting furniture is not always an easy task, but if you're willing to work hard and are able to organize, this could be a great business for you. Some of the advantages of starting such a company are that you can easily begin by working alone, your overhead costs are relatively low, and the physical labor makes for a great workout. As long as dirt and grime exist, there will be a need for your service.

HOW TO GET STARTED

1. Begin by putting together your basic cleaning kit using the following checklist:
   - Sponges
   - Towels and dusting rags
   - Broom and dustpan
   - Vacuum cleaner
   - Mop
   - Glass cleaner
   - Scouring powder
   - Bathroom tile and porcelain cleaner
   - Ammonia

- Floor cleaner
- Furniture polish
- Wood soap
- Feather duster
- Spray bottles
- Cleaning smock (optional)

You can add your own favorite cleaning products to this basic list. The best place to buy your supplies is from a janitorial supply house where you'll save money by buying larger containers of cleaning products.

2. Conduct a trial run by cleaning your own home. You should time yourself and note the amount of cleansers you use for each task. This will help you in figuring out what sort of fees to charge. For example, if it takes you five hours to do a basic cleaning on your own home, you might want to charge $10 an hour for a similar home of a client.

3. Make a list of the cleaning services that you provide. With each new client, find out exactly what they need and expect from you. Have the customer pick out the items they want done weekly or biweekly. Always be sure to find out if they have any special cleaning tasks that they'd like done or if they have some particular item or area in their home that they don't want you to handle. Mrs. Jones might not want you to dust her antique flower vase and Mr. Smith might prefer that you not straighten up or touch a single scrap of paper in his home office. Catering to the wishes of your clients is as important as a good cleaning job and will earn you loyal and happy customers.

4. After your first cleaning, leave a survey card for your client to fill out that asks them if everything was done satisfactorily and if it met their expectations. Most likely, they will jot down a few comments about something that wasn't done quite right. Don't take it personally, but use the information so you can correct and improve your service on the next visit. They will appreciate that you cared enough to ask.

OTHER IDEAS

Green Cleaning

With today's growing concerns about protecting the environment and the harmful effects of chemicals, an all-natural cleaning service just might be a big hit in your neighborhood. The term "green" refers to products and actions that help protect the Earth and its inhabitants. There are many types of all-natural, chemical- and cruelty-free cleaning products on the market today that can be found in health food stores. Such a service would be particularly appealing to sensitive allergy sufferers, families with newborns, and to the growing numbers of citizens concerned with environmental issues. You might consider becoming a part-time distributor of green cleaning products so that your clients will be able to handle everyday tasks in between your visits.

Spring Cleaning Special

Spring cleaning is a term that refers to heavy cleaning done once a year, particularly after winter to remove the past year's buildup of dirt within the home. This type of cleaning can, of course, be done at any time of the year. It usually involves heavy-duty tasks such as steam cleaning carpets and upholstery, cleaning windows and drapery, stripping floors, and moving and cleaning beneath furniture. Many of your clients would be happy to pay for this extra service once a year.

HOUSE PAINTING

Start up cost: $200–$600.

Equipment needed: Extension ladder, step ladder, vehicle equipped to carry supplies, paint rollers and brushes in assorted sizes, drop cloths or plastic sheeting, paint trays, paint thinner (for cleaning brushes), masking tape, rubber gloves, sandpaper, brush comb, pails, and face mask.

Whether you are painting the exterior or interior of a home, a house painting business can be quite profitable. Painting surfaces such as walls and woodwork creates a seal that bonds itself to the surface, forming a film that protects and beautifies. You'll need to learn about the many different types of paints available on the market and decide which will be the best for each job.

INTERIOR PAINTING

When painting the inside of a home, you'll need the basic equipment listed above and a good paint that is specifically designed for interior surfaces.

1. Clean all surfaces that you will be painting, making sure that they are free of grease, dirt, and debris. You might need to sand down old, peeling paint or fill in any holes or cracks with putty. The surface needs to be clean and smooth before you apply the paint.
2. Paint a small area as a test patch and let it dry to make sure that the color is right.
3. Cover all furniture, floors, windows, light switches, electrical outlets, and other items in the home that are in

danger of being splattered with paint. Use your drop cloths or plastic for this, and secure them with masking tape.

EXTERIOR PAINTING

When painting the outside of a home, choose a paint designed for exterior surfaces. You will need some additional tools that are not listed above. These items are a paint scraper, steel wool, electric paint remover, rough surface paint brush, power sander, paint sprayer (optional), and a caulking gun. You will need to diagnose the condition of the home and determine what work needs to be done before you begin painting. You might find peeling old paint, blistering, stains, mildew, or a number of other problems. There are many books available on the subject of painting that will tell you how to correct such problems and perform a professional paint job.

1. Clean and/or repair the outside surface in preparation for painting. Make sure that the surface is dry.

2. Paint a small area as a test patch and let it dry to make sure that the color is right.

3. If you are painting the entire exterior of a house, start from the top and work your way down. Paint the siding first and the trim last.

OTHER IDEAS

- Study the subject of painting by reading books that are available in the library or in bookstores. Also read the manufacturer's instructions about paint and painting tools.

INSURANCE VIDEO-TAPING SERVICE

Start up cost: $800.

Equipment needed: Good color video camera, blank video-tapes, bond.

In this business you'll have two types of clients: home-owners and insurance companies. Basically, you'll use a video camera to tape the contents in a home. Homeowners will use the service to prove that they are in possession of insured items such as valuables. Many insurance companies will hire you on a freelance basis to go to homeowners to verify that their insured belongings actually exist. You can also go and videotape damage to homes caused by disasters such as fires, earthquakes, hurricanes, floods, and tornadoes. Insurance companies now require this when a homeowner makes a claim.

HOW TO GET STARTED

1. Purchase a good color video camera and brush up on your skills so that you're able to capture the best images possible.
2. Send out a mailing or call insurance companies letting them know about your services.
3. Advertise your services to homeowners, particularly those in affluent or disaster-prone areas.
4. Tape the outside of the home, being sure to get the address on tape, then walk through the home taping all items. Have the homeowner take you for a tour and tape all valuable items and/or damage. Make sure that your camera

has a microphone so that your voice can be heard on the tape pointing out what each item is.

TIPS

- Many insurance companies will require you to carry a bond. Check your local Yellow Pages under "Bonds" for information about obtaining one.
- Always make a copy of the videotape for yourself in case a dispute arises. Make sure that each tape is clearly marked with the customer's name, address, and date of the taping.

KEY DUPLICATION SERVICE

Start up cost: $1,500.

Equipment needed: Key cutting machine, blank keys in an assortment of sizes and types.

Everyone needs an extra set of keys, whether for their home, office, or car. You can start your own key duplication service and have a booming business in no time. Duplicate keys usually sell for $2 to $3 each. After making and selling your first thousand or so, you should be able to make back your initial investment. You might be able to find a key machine manufacturer who will lease you a key making machine if you can't afford to buy right now.

HOW TO GET STARTED

1. Look in the Yellow Pages for key making machines. If you can't find a listing, go to a key shop and ask the owner or manager where he purchased his. When you purchase a key cutting machine it will come with complete operating instructions and safety guidelines.

2. Look for a place to set up your shop. You won't need a large space to operate out of, so your rent should be very reasonable. You might consider renting out a space in an established business like a hardware store where your clientele will be automatic.

3. Have a large sign made up that says "Keys" or "Keys Made Here." Being visible is very important in this business.

Many of your customers will be driving by and remember that they need to get a key made.

TIP

- You can sell key accessories such as key chains, key rings, color-coded covers, and magnetic "hide a key" boxes to make an extra profit.

LADIES' RESALE CLOTHING

Start up cost: About $300.

Equipment needed: Clothing racks, folding card table, iron, ironing board, sewing kit, and stock of clothing.

Everyone loves a bargain! Resale clothing is very popular these days, from funky thrift shop items to flashy designer garments. One woman in Los Angeles started a resale clothing business by selling garments at flea markets and swap meets. Within months, she'd made enough money with her part-time sales to open her own boutique. If you love clothing and bargain hunting, this might be a good business for you to get into.

HOW TO GET STARTED

1. Snoop around your local thrift shops and you'll be amazed at the treasures hanging on the racks. You might find a designer blouse for $3 or a 1950s poodle skirt in perfect condition for a mere $5. Consider the resale value of these items. You can probably get $10 for the blouse and up to $40 for the classic skirt. Another place to pick up bargains is at garage sales. With today's fashion rules changing every few months, many people clean out their closets and off-load perfectly good garments that they've grown tired of. Take a look in your own closet as well. You might find a few items that can be added to your resale collection.

2. Pick an item to specialize in, be it vintage clothing or upscale ladies' apparel. I recently met a woman who sells only 1960s handbags and hats. She makes several hundred

dollars profit every weekend at flea markets. Another woman I met specializes in "hardly used" women's business clothing. She has a large selection of suits, blouses, skirts, and belts. She told me that she passes out cards to women in the downtown office district, inviting them to her upcoming flea market shows.

3. Get your stock organized. Iron all of your garments and check to be sure that each piece of clothing looks neat and attractive. Tag each item with a price and its size.

4. Reserve a space at a flea market or swap meet. Look in your local paper for listings of upcoming shows. It is usually necessary to register in advance, and a space costs between $15 and $85.

5. Arrive at the flea market early in the morning to get set up. Display your clothing so that it looks organized. Try putting that vintage, rhinestone-studded evening gown on a mannequin to attract attention to your space. Another good way to attract business is to bring along a portable radio so that you can play music. You'll also find that your card table is an invaluable necessity. Cover it with a nice table cloth and use it to display accessories such as jewelry, belts, and purses. Finally, be sure to have some small bills on you so that you'll be able to make change for your customers.

6. Have business cards made up with your name and phone number on them. You might develop a following of women who like your stock and will want to stop by your booth at your next show.

THE RULES OF RESALE

- Never buy anything that is stained or damaged beyond repair. Unless you can fix that broken zipper or mend that little tear, don't bother with it.
- Ask yourself this question when considering buying an item, "Would I or someone that I know wear this?"

- Try to buy in different sizes. Larger clothing is more difficult to find, especially plus sizes, and if you can find it, you can probably sell it.
- You should resell an item for 50 percent more than you paid for it. For example, if that great little dress costs $7 and you think that you can sell it for $14, you've found yourself a great deal.
- You'll do the best by selling the type of clothing that you like.
- Shop at the larger thrift shops and check them for new stock every couple of days. Get to the shops early in the morning so that you'll have first pick.
- Talk to other people who are selling used clothing. They'll usually be willing to tell you what kind of items they've found to be hot sellers in recent months.

OTHER IDEAS

Wedding Gowns

Resale wedding gowns are always a hot item. You can pick them up at thrift shops or by putting a classified ad in the paper reading, "Will pay cash for used wedding gowns." You'll be surprised at the number of women willing to part with their special white dresses for a little green.

Maternity Clothing

Maternity clothes are another big-selling item for expecting mothers. No one wants to pay full price for a whole new wardrobe that won't fit in nine months! Try placing a classified ad reading, "I buy maternity clothes."

Children's Clothing

Many mothers would consider you a godsend if you specialized in children's resale clothing. Nice children's apparel can be found in thrift shops. Be sure that it's in good condition and always organize your items by size. Anyone who's ever had a garage sale will tell you that one of the first things to go is children's clothing.

Adding Your Own Touch

If you're handy with a needle and thread, you can easily increase the value of your items by adding a little lace or sewing on a few sequins here and there. A silk rose tacked onto a funky old hat can bring in five times what you paid for it. Visit your local fabric or craft store to get supplies and ideas.

Sewing Classes

Taking a sewing class would be a wise investment if you're going to enter the clothing business. From a sewing class you'll learn the skills of stitching and mending and you'll be able to repair your clothing and update old styles. Most community colleges offer beginning level classes. One woman I met has been selling pants that she makes herself out of fancy, antique drapery fabric and she's making a fortune doing it.

Hanging in There

Don't get discouraged if you don't make a million dollars on your first weekend. Hang in there and keep trying. Many successful flea marketers will tell you about good days and bad days. Keep a list of those items that you sold so that you'll have a better idea of what people are looking for and will buy next time.

LOCAL NEWS CLIPPING SERVICE

Start up cost: $100 (for copies).

Equipment needed: None.

A news clipping service sorts through newspapers and magazines and cuts out articles that pertain to needs of its clients, whether it be a mention of the company name or information relating to their field of business. It would be impossible for one person to sort through the thousands of publications put out daily in the country, but you can easily start your own local clipping service, checking the area news for items of interest to your clients. Newspaper clippings are used by businesses and organizations in their promotion and advertising and to track trends in their field of expertise.

HOW TO GET STARTED

1. Contact local businesses that might have a need for your services and ask to speak to the marketing or PR department. Find out what sort of articles or mentions they're looking for and give them a price. Find out how far back they're looking for articles, like one year, five years, and so on. Ask if they only want clippings that mention their company or if they're also interested in articles pertaining to their field of business. Your fee should be based per project or per hour.

2. Go to the library and start your search using the microfiche files. The main library in your area should have the local newspapers on file with articles that date back many

years. Make copies of the articles, ensuring that they're clear and readable. Include any photos that go along with the article.

TIPS

- When delivering articles to clients, always include the entire article and a copy of the newspaper or magazine banner with the date on it.
- Offer your clients a weekly news check where you'll clip articles for them and send them in weekly.

LOCAL TOUR GUIDE

Start up cost: $100.

Equipment needed: Brochures, in some cases a vehicle.

Is there anything unique, historical, or interesting about your city? If so, you can get into the tour business and cash in. Tours are a welcome business in most cities because they boost the local economy by providing restaurants, hotels, and shops with new business.

A woman in Nevada started a tour that greatly increased local business. She lived in an old mining town that was sparsely populated and had a depressed economy. Using her imagination and a little local folklore, she started a tour of haunted buildings in the town. The tour soon became popular with out-of-town guests and all of the local business owners welcomed her tour (and the tourists' dollars) with open arms. A man in Northern California regularly gives a "survival tour" in the wilderness surrounding his home town. He takes tourists on a two-hour walk through the forest, pointing out what kinds of plants are edible and which ones aren't.

Many towns across the country offer unique tours, like "Los Angeles Neon," which is a night time tour of the city's spectacular neon lights. Some cities feature chartered boats where tourists can watch whales. Most towns have something interesting about them that others would want to see.

HOW TO GET STARTED

1. Research the history of your town by reading old newspapers or periodicals at the library in order to come up with an interesting angle for a tour.

2. Once you've established what sort of tour you'd like to host, check with the occupants of the buildings you'll visit, if applicable, to make sure that they'd like to be an attraction.

3. Alert your local city visitor's information center of your tour so that they can refer business to you.

4. Make up some nice brochures about your tour and leave them at city offices, restaurants, and hotels.

5. If you need a vehicle to conduct your tour, such as a passenger van or boat, you should consider renting or chartering one until you can afford to purchase your own.

6. Have your tour meet in a centrally located place close to shopping and hotels. Your tour should end at the same place it started.

TIPS

- Make sure that your guests are comfortable and have access to bathrooms and snacks.
- Make sure that your tour isn't too long or boring. After all, you're being paid to entertain. Test it out on some friends before charging strangers for it. Encourage your friends to ask questions so that you can be prepared with answers.

MAILING LIST CREATION

Start up cost: $100.

Equipment needed: Card table, wooden box with a slot in the top, pencils, name cards.

Businesses like to have a large database of potential customers for their products or services. They often mail out catalogs and promotional pieces to advertise specials and increase their business. You can start a mailing list service that caters to particular businesses and make a nice profit for yourself. The best way to get names of people interested in your client's product or service is by having a contest where a prize is given to the lucky winner.

HOW TO GET STARTED

1. Contact local businesses. Let's use a golf shop as an example. Call or visit the golf shop and tell them that you can help them expand their business by creating a new mailing list. The shop will need to donate some sort of prize, like a new set of golf clubs or a gift certificate to their store.

2. Tell them that you charge a certain fee for each name that you deliver to them.

3. Have some small cards made up where the contestants can fill out their name, address, and phone number. Set up your card table and wooden box in front of the store itself, at a local golf course, or anyplace you might find people interested in the golf shop. Have a large sign by your booth that says, "Win a Free Set of Golf Clubs! Enter Here." Have people fill out the name cards and drop them in the box.

You'll probably get more names if you have the prize at your booth for them to see.

4. Deliver the name cards to your client and collect your fee. Make sure that the shop picks a winner from the names and delivers the prize.

The golf shop now has a list of names of people who are interested in golf clubs. You can hold similar contests for almost any business. Restaurants might offer a free dinner for two while a carpet cleaner might offer a free cleaning.

MAIL-ORDER BOOKLETS

Start up cost: $200 (for copying and initial advertising).

Equipment needed: None (although a home computer would be useful for page layout and design).

Information sells. Thousands of people send off for mail-order booklets every day, and you can also cash in on this booming business by selling your ideas through mail order. Do you know how to do something special or have some information that would be valuable to others? Some of the booklets that are selling cover making money, recipes, caring for pets, improving your home, crafts, car care, and saving money. While the cost of getting a small booklet printed can be as little as 10¢ per copy, they can be resold for $5 or more.

HOW TO GET STARTED

1. Choose your subject and research it well. You want to provide the reader with as much information as possible.

2. Write your booklet. Use a word processor or have it typeset so that it looks professional.

3. Include illustrations in your booklet if you can. You can buy books of copyright-free art at art supply stores.

4. Have your booklet printed. The most common and cost-effective way is to have your booklet copied or printed onto white, $8\frac{1}{2} \times 11$-inch paper that will be folded in half. Choose colorful card stock paper as your cover and use two staples to secure the cover and pages in place.

5. Advertise your booklet in newspapers and magazines in the classified section. Use catchy and interesting phrases

like, "secrets revealed." Also, offer a 30-day money-back guarantee.

6. List a P.O. box address for your orders. Check your mail daily and fill all orders immediately.

TIP

- Always copyright your work when selling written material.

MARKET RESEARCH SURVEY

Start up cost: $100 for initial advertising.

Equipment needed: Telephone and/or clipboards.

Have you ever seen an advertisement where the manufacturer states something like, "Four out of five dentists surveyed said that Sparkle Toothpaste makes your teeth whiter than other leading brands"? The statistical information most likely came from a marketing research survey. Research surveys are in great demand in today's competitive business world. Starting your own marketing research business is as easy as picking up your phone or visiting your neighbor.

HOW TO GET STARTED

1. Contact local businesses and let them know about your services. Work with your client to develop a survey that will provide marketable information for him or her. For example, you might be hired by a local car dealership. You can call all of their previous customers and ask survey questions like, "Are you happy with your vehicle?" or "How was the service at Star Motors?" Tabulate the information in an easy to understand format and deliver it to your client. The dealership can now honestly say something like "Over 500 satisfied customers since 1988" or "Providing the friendliest service in town."

2. Another angle to take in this business is to find out what the public wants. You might be hired by an Italian restaurant so that they can find out how to get more business. By telephoning 100 residents of the city and asking,

"What do you want from an Italian restaurant?" you might find that the number one answer is "home delivery" or "Italian ice deserts." The restaurant can now use this information to their advantage and increase their business by providing what the public wants.

3. Surveys can be conducted by telephone by using the phone book or customer lists provided by your client. You can also make up a survey, get it photocopied, and have people fill them out at grocery stores, malls, and so on.

TIPS

- Always be polite and courteous to the people that you're surveying.
- Most people will be happy to answer your questions as long as they're brief and to the point. People generally like to voice their opinions.

MESSANGER/
ERRAND SERVICE

Start up cost: Under $500.

Equipment needed: Reliable vehicle, answering machine, and pager.

A messenger/errand service is one of the easiest businesses to start. It is also popular with businesses and people with busy lives, as you'll soon find out. Some of the advantages of starting this business are that it can be easily started from home, can be run by one person, and can have an unlimited potential for expansion.

A young woman I know, Mary, started her own messenger company. She had been wanting to get into business for herself, but didn't have any money. She came up with the brilliant idea to start an errand service in her city.

Mary made up some flyers and began passing them out to local businesses and to homes in the more affluent part of her neighborhood. *The very next day* she found herself delivering parcels, running errands, and *making money*. She had started her own company and had gotten it off the ground in a matter of hours!

In the beginning, she admitted that it was quite a juggling act. Mary was operating the company alone, which made her the delivery person, receptionist, accountant, and advertising executive. She handled the random activity by turning on her answering machine when she was out of the office. Her answering machine then referred callers to her pager so that she could receive messages while out in the field. At night she organized her paperwork and balanced the company checkbook while dreaming up new ways to advertise her service.

Within a few weeks her hard work began to pay off because she had built up a base of regular clients who used her services several times a week. Additionally, she was continually picking up new customers. Mary then hired several delivery people and was able to stay in the office and dispatch calls to her drivers.

Mary agreed that this type of company is perfect for the eager entrepreneur who doesn't have a lot of money to get started.

HOW TO START YOUR OWN SERVICE

1. Decide what kind of service you want to operate: Errand services usually cater to the personal needs of busy people, while messenger/delivery services cater to the needs of businesses.

Your errand service might offer the following services:

- Grocery shopping
- Gift shopping
- Bank deposits
- Dry cleaning drop-off/pickup
- Personal parcel delivery
- Video rental
- Post office visits
- Prescription pickup
- DMV (Department of Motor Vehicles) visits

Your messenger/delivery service might offer the following services:

- Parcel pickup/delivery (such as copies, documents, supplies, etc.)
- Lunch pickup and delivery
- Travel agency pickups

- Permit filing
- Flower/gift delivery
- Post office visits

2. If you are starting your business alone, you'll need to set up your answering machine and get a pager until you can afford to hire a driver and receptionist. Your recording should say something like this: "Hello. You've reached Errand Express. We're out of the office right now, but please leave a message. If you need immediate service, please page at us at 213-555-5555. Your call will be returned within thirty minutes. Thank you for choosing Errand Express." Your clients will either leave a message or page you. Be sure to check your machine frequently and always return your pages within thirty minutes.

3. Study maps of your city and get familiar with alternate routes and short cuts. By saving time you'll have more room in your schedule.

You'll find that the best way to charge for this type of service is a combination of time and mileage, for example $20 an hour and 20¢ per mile. If it takes you an hour to pick up a package from your client's office and deliver it to his accountant downtown, and you drove twenty-four miles, the charge would be $24.80 based on this formula. If applicable, add parking fees and waiting time into your charge. You can also offer after-hours emergency service and almost double your hourly rates. Always give your client an estimate before starting a job, and keep your calculator nearby.

TIP

- In some cities and counties it is necessary to get a permit from the Department of Transportation if you are going to be using public freeways and roads to conduct your business. Call or visit your local office to find out what is required in your area.

OTHER IDEAS

- With this type of business the sources of work are almost unlimited. You can approach businesses such as flower shops, travel agencies, markets, and restaurants offering your delivery service. You can also cater to the needs of specific fields of business such as architects or realtors. Find out what is needed from each field. Also see the listing in this book on the Permit Filing Service.

MIDDLEMAN ADVERTISING

Start up cost: None to minimal.

Equipment needed: None.

Do you have what it takes to make some serious money? The following advertising business is an extremely hot idea that a friend of mine told me about just weeks ago. The possibilities are boundless. A man started up a company recently that grew from a small operation into a multimillion dollar business almost overnight!

HERE'S HOW HE GOT STARTED

1. First, he went into his local pharmacy and approached the owner, offering to sell him a year's supply of the white paper bags that hold prescriptions for an incredibly low price. The bags would have the pharmacist's name and business address printed on them. This of course interested the pharmacist because he uses thousands of bags a year and has to pay an arm and a leg to have them printed.

2. Now that the deal was closed with the pharmacist to purchase the bags, the man made visits to local business owners (restaurants, dry cleaners, dentists, etc.) offering them a year's supply of advertising at an incredibly low rate.

3. How was he able to offer these services to the pharmacist and the local businesses and still make a profit? Simple. The man had coupons for the local businesses printed on the pharmacist's bags! The businesses that advertised on the bags paid a fair fee and the pharmacist was happy both to have a year's supply of bags and to support to his neighbors

by passing out hundreds of coupons daily (via the bags). The operation fed itself, leaving quite a bit of profit for the middleman who dreamed up the idea.

4. It all went so well for him that he hired a sales crew to continue the operation in other cities across the country.

The possibilities with this type of advertising business are unlimited. All you need to do is get creative and establish relationships between the stores, advertisers, and a printer. Is your pharmacist still using plain white bags?

OTHER IDEAS

- Why not use the steps above but with grocery receipt tapes? All stores give out receipts and the blank side would be a great place to print coupons.

MINIATURE MAILING HOUSE

Start up cost: None.

Equipment needed: None.

Many businesses and organizations are effectively using third-class bulk mail to advertise their products and services. The United States Postal Service offers customers using their third-class mail service rates specially discounted to a fraction of regular postage prices. To qualify for these special rates, businesses and organizations must have a permit from the post office. By walking businesses through the permit forms and then preparing your customer's third-class mailings, you can start a miniature mailing house from your own home.

At first glance, preparing a third-class mailing appears to be confusing. The postal service has come out with a free publication that walks you through each step of putting a mailing together. It is a booklet titled *Third-Class Mail Preparation* and can be picked up at any post office in the bulk mail department.

HOW TO START A MAILING HOUSE

1. Study the information from the post office on third-class mailings until you fully understand how to do a mailing. If you have specific questions, visit your local post office and speak to a representative.

2. Approach businesses (preferably small ones to begin with) and let them know about your mailing house. Tell them your prices based on the cost of the mailing plus an

additional fee for yourself. This additional fee will be your payment for preparing the mailing.

3. Have your new customers fill out the forms that the post office requires and get their bulk mail permit if they don't already have one.

4. Determine whether your customer already has a mailing list or if one needs to be bought. (There are many services that have mailing lists available for sale that target a specific market.)

5. Have the customer get their bulk-mail piece printed.

6. Stuff, label, sort, and deliver the mailing to the post office.

TIPS

- Make sure that you can handle the amount of mail you'll be sending out, especially if you're working alone.
- Give your customers a reasonable delivery date to the post office once you have received the piece from the printer.

MOBILE AUTO BODY AND DENT REPAIR

Start up cost: $500.

Equipment needed: See listing below.

Finding your clientele is as easy as spotting a dent on a car. Every time you see a dented vehicle, go over and talk to the owner and recruit him on the spot. If the owner isn't present, leave one of your business cards on the windshield. Most jobs can be completed in twenty minutes to four hours. The best clientele for this business is people with automobiles three years old or older who can't afford to take their car to an expensive body shop.

A friend of mine makes a great living doing on-the-spot body repairs. He told me about a client of his whose two front fenders were badly dented. The client had gotten estimates of over $600 to repair this older-model car. The car was only worth $1,100 and she didn't want to put that kind of money into it, yet the fenders were an eyesore. My friend repaired her fenders by applying Bondo, sanding, priming, and painting the damage all for under $200 and using less than $20 in materials and three hours of his time. The customer was extremely pleased and my friend was paid handsomely for his time as well as receiving ten other referrals from his happy customer. He told me that with a little experience, you'll get the feel for how much work is involved in any body repair situation and learn time-saving tricks.

HOW TO GET STARTED

1. The easiest way to learn the basics of the trade is by reading books and pamphlets on the subject and practicing

on the cars of friends, neighbors, and relatives. You might also consider apprenticing at a local body shop for a few weeks to learn the basics.

2. Put together a kit of basic tools and materials with the following items:

- Dent pulling slide hammer
- Five different types of body hammers
- Three rubber mallets of differing sizes
- Four or five hammer dollies
- Several crow bars of differing sizes
- Floor jack and bottle jack
- Plenty of Bondo
- Several tubes of body putty
- Assorted metal and plastic putty spatulas
- Sand paper
- Disc sander
- Hand block sander
- Assortment of wet and dry sandpaper and emory cloth
- Assorted cheese graters
- Metal chisels
- Set of hand tools (screwdrivers, wrenches, hammer, etc.)
- Extension cords
- Paint primer
- Spray paint (assorted colors)
- Masking tape
- Rolls of plastic and newspapers
- Dust pan and broom
- Cleanup solvent
- Hand cleaner and paper towels
- Shop towels and rags
- Plenty of business cards

3. Go out and find your first client. The world is full of potential customers who can be found anywhere that you

find cars. Try looking for them at gas stations, shopping mall parking lots, driveways, parks, and office buildings. It is best to do the work on the spot if possible. Generally, if the customer is happy with your work, you'll get enough referrals to keep you busy from there on out.

MOBILE DOG AND CAT GROOMING

Start up cost: $300.

Equipment needed: Electric razor, scissors, dog and cat shampoo, flea shampoo, gloves, animal nail clippers, dog and cat brushes, buckets, and vehicle.

Mobile pet grooming is a nice service to provide to your community. Many people don't have the time to take their pets to the groomer and therefore appreciate the convenience of a groomer coming to their home. This is a perfect business for animal lovers. Before you start, you should learn about grooming techniques for different dog and cat breeds. There are books available on the subject at bookstores and libraries. When you've finished a job for a client, set up another appointment to come back in a month or so while you're there. You'll have a lot of repeat business if you do a good job.

TIPS

- Talk to the owners of local pet shops and to veterinarians (who don't offer grooming services) and ask if you can leave some of your business cards on their counter.
- Never groom a sick, injured, or badly flea-bitten pet. Advise the owner to take the animal to a veterinarian.

MOTHER'S HELPER SERVICE

Start up cost: None.

Equipment needed: None.

After having a baby, many women need a little extra help with housework and with their new baby until they can recover and get back on their feet, particularly after a difficult birth. Starting a helper service for new moms is a great way to make a living if you like babies and temporary assignments. With this type of business, you help your clients with housework, cooking, diaper changing, errands, shopping, and anything else that is needed. Although it isn't mandatory, you should look into taking a CPR class. You will not be providing any medical services, just helping make the new mother's life a little easier for a week or so until she's feeling better.

There are many ways to find clients in this business. Get some business cards or flyers made up and leave them in places where mothers-to-be can see them, such as hospital bulletin boards, maternity shops, baby furniture shops, and doctors' offices (with permission first).

TIPS

- Have a list of references available for your clients to call before they hire you.
- Do everything possible to make the new mother comfortable.
- Have a list of emergency numbers handy in case you need to call the doctor, hospital, or family members.

NEIGHBORHOOD INFORMATION SERVICE

Start up cost: None.

Equipment needed: Computer (not mandatory, but it will be extremely useful).

If you've ever moved into a new neighborhood, you'll recognize the value of this service. Do you recall having to search for a dentist, doctor, school, bookstore, restaurant, or hair salon? By doing a little research in your own neighborhood (and others), you can create a priceless gold mine of data.

HOW TO GET STARTED

1. Nobody knows the neighborhood like somebody who lives in it, so start your project in town. Pretend you've just moved there and don't know anything about the area. Start by making a list of all the services you might need: doctor, dentist, veterinarian, grocery store, hair salon, barber, schools, chimney sweep, gardener, plumber, restaurants, auto mechanic, stationer, and shopping malls.

2. Make a list of the best shops and services that you know of, noting the quality of the service or product. List the names and addresses of each and any other additional information. For example:

- Chinese restaurant:
  The Red Dragon
  1234 California Ave.
  Glendale, CA 90505
  (818) 555-1212

The Red Dragon serves excellent authentic Chinese cuisine. The restaurant was established in 1960 and is run by the owner, Lee Chan. They deliver within a five-mile radius at no extra charge.

- Plumbing
  Jack's Plumbing
  P.O. Box 333
  Glendale, CA 90505
  (818) 555-3333

  Jack Wilson is the owner of this company established in 1976. He runs a team of honest, reliable plumbers. His prices are fair and he offers 24-hour emergency service.

3. Once you have a file of all of the companies and businesses you wish to list, organize them alphabetically and make copies. Call local real estate agents and tell them about your information package and suggest that it would be a great item for new families moving into the area. Sell your information packages to the real estate agents at a fair price.

OTHER IDEAS

- Make up a free neighborhood guide and solicit local businesses to advertise in it for a fee. Get the guide printed up and leave copies in local stores, doctors' offices, and even the city hall. The advertising fee from the local businesses should cover the costs of printing and leave enough left over for you to make a nice little profit. Put out a new, updated guide every six months or so.
- Try the same process in another town.

NIGHT CLUB AND RESTAURANT SALES

Start up cost: $100.

Equipment needed: Instant camera and film, and/or flowers, bucket, and cellophane wrap.

Thousands of people go out to night clubs and restaurants. These places are a gold mine for a roaming photographer or flower salesperson. Couples and large groups celebrating birthdays will be your best customers.

INSTANT PHOTOS

Who ever thought you could make a living with an instant camera? The procedure is easy and fast. Simply approach patrons inside the establishment and ask them if they'd like a photo to remember the evening. Take the photo and let it develop. Then place it inside a photo card. (Photo cards are similar to a greeting card but with a slot to insert a photo. They can be purchased or you can make them yourself out of card-stock paper.) Most people will pay up to $5 for a picture.

FLOWERS

Flowers are a hot item, especially for couples who forgot to get flowers for each other. All you need to do is buy some fresh flowers (roses and carnations will sell best), garnish a single flower with baby's breath, then wrap it in cellophane. Carry your wrapped flowers in a bucket and approach couples inside or outside restaurants or night clubs. This item will also sell for up to $5.

TIPS

- Owners of night clubs will usually let you inside at no charge since you will be providing a service for their customers. All you need to do is ask.
- Bring along enough cash to make change for your customers.
- Another good location for taking instant photos is at local tourist attractions.

ORNAMENTAL POND BUILDING

Start up cost: $100 (not including pond building materials, which vary in price).

Equipment needed: Vehicle to carry large loads (a pickup truck would be ideal), shovels in various sizes, and measuring tape.

Adding a small pond in the backyard or garden adds beauty and value to a home. Most ponds require little maintenance and will last for many years. Prefabricated pond liners can be purchased at most garden centers or you can easily create an original design. Water plants, fish, decorative stones, lighting, and waterfalls can all be easily installed.

HOW TO GET STARTED

Meet with your customer and discuss what type and size pond they want. Decide on a location. If you plan to install any features that require electricity, make sure that the location the customer has chosen is close to a power supply. Using a rope, lay out the shape on the future pond site to make sure that the customer is happy with the design.

PREFABRICATED PONDS

The easiest type of pond to install is prefabricated. They are less likely to leak than a concrete pond and are made out of durable plastic, rubber, or vinyl. They come in many shapes and sizes and can be bought at garden centers or directly from their manufacturers.

With this type of pond, you simply dig a hole to fit the preformed pond, fill the bottom of the hole with a thin layer of sand, and set the pond liner in place. Fill the pond with water and add a submersible pump. Decorate the edges with stones or tiles set in mortar.

BUILDING A POND FROM SCRATCH

This type of pond is also called a liner pond. By choosing this type of pond, you have more freedom to create custom shapes for your customer. As with the prefabricated type, you dig a hole (about 8 inches deep) in the desired shape. Spread a thin layer of sand in the bottom of the pond and lay down a plastic sheet of pond liner that completely covers the hole. Fill the pond with water and install decorative stones around the sides.

Submersible pumps are necessary to keep the pond clean and clear. They can be bought at garden centers. Follow the manufacturer's installation instructions. Waterfalls, lighting, water plants, and fountains can also be purchased at garden centers.

TIP

- Information about building ponds is available at garden centers and in landscaping books.

OUTDOOR LIGHT INSTALLATION

Start up cost: $100.

Equipment needed: Outdoor lighting kits (available at larger hardware stores or they can be ordered directly from the manufacturer).

The benefits of having a system of low-voltage outdoor lights are security, safety, beauty, and economy. Many homeowners have outdoor lighting systems to spotlight entryways, outline pools, illuminate trees, brighten patios, and make sidewalks and walkways safer and easier to see. Installation is fast and easy.

HOW TO GET STARTED

1. Go to your local hardware store and research the different types of outdoor lights available and find out what the going rate is for kits. You'll find the prices to be surprisingly affordable.

2. Contact the manufacturer and ask for their catalog. There are many different styles of lights, all of which create a different effect. You can also order books from the manufacturer that will give you helpful hints on installation and maintenance.

3. After you've received your materials from the manufacturer, come up with your pricing guidelines. Advertise your services and offer free estimates.

4. When giving an estimate, find out what kind of effect the customer wants to create. Bring along a product brochure and pick out the style of lights that best suit the customer's

needs. Measure the yard or area you'll be installing the system in and figure out how many lights and how much cable you'll need for the job. Draw up a customized lighting plan. Give the customer a price, and set up an appointment to do the work.

OTHER IDEAS

- Special timers and movement sensors that automatically run the system are available and can be additionally sold to the customer.

PACKING SERVICE

Start up cost: $300.

Equipment needed: Cardboard boxes, packing tape, bubble wrap, newspaper, large black markers, furniture dolly.

Thousands of people move from one house to another every year. Most people can't stand to move and are happy to pay for a service to handle the packing for them. Moving companies generally just move the items out, so you'll have relatively little competition with this business. A packing service securely wraps and packs the belongings of their clients in preparation for a move.

HOW TO GET STARTED

1. You'll need to purchase packing supplies. See the list above for the basic materials you'll need.

2. Learn about packing procedures. Some rental truck and moving companies offer free literature and videos about safe and efficient packing.

3. When packing for a client, mark every box with a complete listing of the items inside. You should also write the destination of the box on the outside, such as "kitchen."

4. Advertise your services to homeowners. Give some of your business cards to moving companies so that they can refer clients to you.

TIPS

- Let local businesses know about your services since they sometimes relocate.
- Send a mailing to local real estate agents with a few of your business cards.

PAPER SHREDDING AND RECYCLING SERVICE

Start up cost: $600.

Equipment needed: Paper shredding machine, vehicle.

Many businesses have an overload of documents that for security reasons can't be thrown in the trash. A mobile document shredding service goes to its clients and shreds their documents on-site, then removes the shredded paper and takes it to a recycling center. You can make a nice profit by charging your clients a fee and then making a little extra cash at the paper recycling center. You can buy a portable paper shredding machine at an office supply store. Start off with a small one if you must and save money to buy a larger one later.

TIPS

- Some of your clients may want you to carry a bond because you'll be dealing with sensitive documents. Call a bond company to purchase one.
- Call your local recycling centers and find out what their rules and regulations are regarding shredded paper.

PATENT SEARCHES

Start up cost: $50 (for photocopying expenses).

Equipment needed: None. (You will need to have access to a large library that has the facilities to conduct a patent search).

A patent is a typed legal document issued by the U.S. Patent Office that gives an inventor exclusive rights to his or her invention. In the United States, a patent expires seventeen years after it has been issued. A patent search is the process of discovering whether an invention has been previously patented by searching through existing patents.

Patent searches are time consuming and many inventors hire services to conduct searches. You may want to work with a patent agent in this business. A patent agent is an individual specifically trained in patent law and procedures. After you conduct a search it would be a good idea to make an arrangement with such an individual to bring copies of your completed search to him or her for legal counsel, thus thoroughly completing a search for your client.

Since the patent search process is long and detailed, the following information is only a brief summary of the process. Free help and information is available at libraries that are set up to conduct patent searches. There are also many books available on patent searches.

HOW TO CONDUCT A
BASIC PATENT SEARCH

1. Figure out what class and subclass the invention falls under. Take a look at the *Index to Classification*, which is a reference book that lists invention types by category.

2. With a list of the possible class and subclass that the invention may fall under, consult the *Manual of Classification*. This is a reference book that serves as a detailed outline of technology by subject of invention. Write down the class and subclass numbers. You may need to look up several subjects before you arrive at the most precise class and subclass for the invention.

3. Look at the Patent Classification Subclass Listing on microfilm and look up each of the class and subclass numbers that you have found. Each class and subclass will list beneath it a list of patents that you will need to look at. Make copies of the microfiche so that you will know what patents to search.

4. Look up each patent number in a publication called the *Official Gazette*. You will find drawings and detailed descriptions of each patent. This publication dates back many years. Make photocopies of similar patents that you find.

5. After searching all patents, bring all of your information and photocopies to a patent agent for counsel.

TIP

- Some libraries now have equipment available to conduct patent searches by computer. Check with the staff for information on how to use this method.

PERMIT FILING SERVICE

Start up cost: $0.

Equipment needed: None.

Filing permits with the city is a needed and extremely valuable service to many professionals. I used to get requests for this when I ran my messenger company and could have had an entire business to handle permit filing alone. Just visit the city building permit office and you'll see what I mean. Frustrated contractors and architects stand in line, anxiously tapping their fingers, wasting their valuable time. Most of these professionals are willing to pay a fee to have someone else do it for them.

HOW TO GET STARTED

1. Get a list of local contractors and send each a letter introducing yourself and your services with your prices. I used to charge $30 per hour to wait in line plus 25¢ per mile. If your local permit office is in a large city, you'll also want to add in the cost of parking, which in my case was an extra $10 on an average day.

2. Tell the contractor up front that he must already have his permits filled out and ready to be filed. Be sure that he also includes a check for filing the permit and that all of the paperwork is signed. Remember, he is paying you to stand in line for him, not to do his job.

3. Pick up the paperwork at the contractor's office and take it to the permit office. Be sure to have the contractor's phone number with you in case you need to call him for

some reason. Once the filing is done, return the receipts and paperwork to the contractor. Have him pay you for your services.

OTHER IDEAS

- As a courtesy, ask the contractor if he needs you to pick up any extra forms while you're down at the permit office. He will appreciate this.
- Leave your business card at building supply stores, blueprint shops, and anyplace else you might find contractors.

PET DETECTIVE

Start up cost: $0.

Equipment: A nose for sniffing out mysteries.

If you've ever lost a pet, you know the heartbreak and worry that it can create. Thousands of animals stray away from home every day and need a good sleuth to reunite them with their families. This is a great part-time service that you can provide to your community.

HOW TO FIND A MISSING PET

1. Check the lost and found section of your local newspaper for missing pet ads.
2. Call up the owners and introduce yourself as a pet detective and explain your services.
3. You'll need to get the following information about the missing animal:

- Pet's name
- Breed and detailed description
- Date the pet was lost
- Location where the pet was last seen
- Age and sex of the pet
- Identifying marks or peculiarities

4. Meet with the owner and ask for a photo of the pet. Make payment arrangements, for example an up-front fee that will cover your advertising and time. Let the owner know that the second half of the payment will be due on the safe return of the pet. Have the owner sign a written agreement with you if you wish.

5. Look around the neighborhood for posted signs stating "found dog or cat" and see if you can find a match to the missing animal. Check the lost and found section of newspapers in the area and call up those ads advertising found pets that are close to the missing animal's profile.

6. Check the local animal pounds for the missing pet.

7. Make up some signs for the missing animal with a description and photo and post them in the neighborhood. Some shop owners may let you place them in their windows.

8. Some cities have papers that offer free ads or you can take out a classified if the customer pays for it in the initial fee.

PET HOTEL

Start up cost: $1,000.

Equipment needed: A large yard and indoor space, feed, and proper cages.

If you love animals, this could be the perfect business for you to start. Most pet owners need to take their beloved animals to a pet hotel at least once every few years when they go on vacation or out of town for business. They want reasonable rates and, most of all, a loving, clean environment for Fido while they're away.

HOW TO GET STARTED

1. You'll need to build roomy, comfortable cages that are sturdy and easy to clean. A large, well-ventilated garage is an ideal place. You'll also need to build some fenced dog runs where the animals can get outside a couple of times a day. A "playroom" is also a great idea in this business: Animals get lonely and frightened when they're away from home and half an hour of individualized attention time can do them a world of good. It's also a great selling point to your customers.

2. Once your hotel rooms have been constructed, you'll need to purchase food and water bowls. You might also offer a menu consisting of several different types of food for dogs and cats. If you want to get fancy, you could offer home baked treats for an extra charge.

3. Visit other pet hotels and kennels to find out what kind of plans they offer and the prices they charge. Figure out your own prices based on the going rates adding in your cost of feed and other expenses.

4. Advertise your services with flyers and classified ads. The local pet shop and veterinarian will probably let you leave some business cards on the counter. You could also make up some "Club Pet Vacation" brochures that will inform customers about the special services your hotel offers.

TIPS

- Be sure to collect payment in advance from the customer. Unfortunately, there are people who will check in their pet and never return to pick him up.
- Check into local laws regarding zoning and permits.

OTHER IDEAS

- Anything that you can do to make your hotel unique will bring in more business. Pretty pictures and brightly painted rooms won't mean a thing to Fluffy, but it might make all of the difference to his owner. How about offering a free stuffed mouse toy to each cat or a tennis balls to the dogs? Little details like this can create confidence in pet owners and make them feel safe leaving their friends with you.
- For an extra charge you could add services such as grooming or special vitamin programs for the animals. Shuttle service from the customer's home could also be added on for an extra fee.

PET TAXI

Start up cost: $200.

Equipment needed: Vehicle large enough to carry cages, pet cages (sizes small, medium, and large), leashes, choke chains (sizes small, medium, and large), and first aid kit.

Animals, like people, need to go places sometimes. A pet taxi service provides safe transportation for animals and takes the burden off owners who either don't have the time or means to take their pet where it needs to go.

A van or large, enclosed vehicle is ideal for this business. You'll need to purchase several cages in large, medium, and small sizes and secure them in the interior of your vehicle to provide a comfortable ride. Having a few spare leashes and collars in various sizes will also come in handy and will ensure that the animal doesn't escape on the trip.

Offer transportation to the veterinarian, groomer, airport, kennel, or wherever else an animal might need to go. It would be a good idea to get some business cards or brochures printed up about your service and leave a stack at the places to which you commonly travel.

Charge your customers by the mile and for waiting time (if requested by the owner). Some pet owners will want you to wait at the veterinarian or handle boarding their pet on an airplane.

TIPS

- Learn about animal first aid procedures and carry a kit of emergency supplies in your vehicle such as bandages and blankets. There are books available on the subject in libraries and bookstores.

- Avoid playing loud music or jolty driving while transporting animals. Animals get spooked and excited easily, especially when they are ill or away from home. By talking to them in a gentle, soothing tone they will feel more comfortable and relaxed.

PLANT CARE

Start up cost: $500.

Equipment needed: Garden sprayer, watering cans, plant food, potting soil, gardening gloves, lambswool duster, leaf shining product, ladder, trash bags, plant clippers, rags, broom, and dust pan.

Mobile plant care services mainly cater to large establishments such as banks, hotels, shopping malls, and office buildings that house a large number of plants for decoration purposes. If you have a green thumb and enjoy gardening, this could be the perfect business for you. These services usually set up accounts with a client and agree to come in once a week to water, feed, and remove dead leaves from plants.

HOW TO GET STARTED

1. Put together a plant care kit including the items listed above and any special products that you wish to add.

2. Contact establishments that house a large number of plants and let them know about your services.

3. Give each client an estimate based on a weekly or biweekly visit, basing your prices on the time you will spend caring for the plants and the supplies you'll use. Work out a contract with your client that specifies the times you will be there and payment arrangements.

4. After finding out what type of plants your client has, educate yourself about the particular species by reading gardening books or by talking to someone at the local plant nursery.

OTHER IDEAS

- In addition to your larger routes, you can offer the additional service of residential "plant sitting" or maintenance. Many people go out of town and need someone to water their plants while they're away.

POOL CLEANING

Start up cost: $400.

Equipment needed: Pool chemicals, skimmer, brushes, and chemical testing kit.

Pool cleaning is a simple and dependable business to get involved in. As long as there are swimming pools, there will be a need for pool cleaners.

HOW TO GET STARTED

1. Educate yourself on pool cleaning by visiting your local pool cleaning supply store or library. You will be able to find ample literature.
2. Once you have become educated on the subject, offer to clean a friend or neighbor's pool as training.
3. When you feel that you are an accomplished pool cleaner, start promoting your services to pool owners. Affluent neighborhoods have a high concentration of pool owners.
4. Set your prices based on your time involved and the supplies you use for each job. Call five to ten other pool cleaning companies to establish what the current price structure is in your area.
5. Set up a schedule with each customer to establish your route.

OTHER IDEAS

- Learn how to repair cracks, tiles, and plaster and learn to maintain pumping equipment. Offer this service to your clients.

- Selling pool accessories such as water heaters, water filters, pool covers, non-slip materials, diving boards, slides, and lighting can bring in an extra profit for your business.
- Aerial maps are a good reference source for locating swimming pools in the area where you want to work. These can be purchased at local map stores.

RAIN GUTTER CLEANING

Start up cost: $200.

Equipment needed: Truck or vehicle equipped to carry a ladder, extension ladder, plastic gutter scoop (available at hardware stores), broom, 4-inch chimney sweeping brush with several flexible extension rods, rags, a long garden hose, bucket, and a pair of heavy-duty work gloves.

Rain gutters are drainage pipes that are installed on the roof around the perimeter of a home to catch rain water and melted snow. The water travels through the gutters and down to the ground through vertical pipes called downspouts. Gutters protect the roof and home from serious water damage. These pipes get clogged with leaves, twigs, dirt, and debris and need to be cleaned out yearly.

Gutter cleaning can be done at any time of the year, although the fall season will probably be the busiest due to falling leaves getting trapped in the pipes. Gutters and downspouts are made of molded vinyl or metal and are either snapped together or sealed in sections with caulking. The cleaning process in either case will be essentially the same.

HOW TO GET STARTED

1. Position your extension ladder firmly against the roof at the highest slope near a downspout. Carry your tools up with you and hang your bucket on the ladder where it can be reached easily. (You can purchase a special hanging bucket at a hardware store.)

2. Use a rag to plug the downspout and begin sweeping the debris from the gutter into a pile. Using your gutter scoop or hands, pick up the pile of debris and put it in your bucket. Work your way down the length of the gutter toward the downspout until it is free of debris. Unplug the downspout and go on to the next section of gutter.

3. When you have cleaned all of the gutters, run water from your hose down each gutter to ensure that there is no blockage. If you find that there is a clog in the downspout, sweep down it with a 4-inch chimney sweeping brush and retest with water again. The water should pass through the pipe easily.

TIP

- You may also install leaf guards for your customers to protect the gutters from clogging until the next cleaning. Leaf guards are wire mesh pieces that cover the top of the gutters and tend to trap leaves and debris on top of them, allowing the water to drain. Leaf guards can be bought at hardware stores or you can make them yourself by cutting strips of galvanized wire mesh with quarter-inch holes to fit over the top of the gutter.

TROUBLESHOOTING

- You may come across leaking or disconnected joints in the gutters or downspouts. Most minor water leaks can be repaired with silicone or vinyl caulking. More serious leaking problems may be caused by rusted metal gutters. New gutters and downspouts can be bought at most hardware stores.

RARE HERB AND PLANT FARMER

Start up cost: $200.

Equipment needed: Seeds, gardening tools.

If you enjoy gardening and being outdoors, this could be the perfect business for you. There are many herbs and plants that are either difficult to obtain or have a high retail price. Some herbs cost over $30 a pound! If you have a large yard or access to a piece of land, you can start your very own farm and turn a nice profit when your crop is ready for market! A man in Arizona made his fortune growing loofahs. Loofahs are plants used as all-natural scrubbing sponges. He simply planted some seeds and waited for his crop to grow. He then began selling his loofahs to several local health food stores.

HOW TO GET STARTED

1. Check with your local health food stores to find out which herbs are the most expensive and/or most difficult to obtain. Make a list of them and find out if the store owner would buy them from you.
2. Contact seed companies and see if they sell seeds for the plants that you want to grow. If they do, find out if that particular species can grow in your area and if it needs any special maintenance or care.
3. Order your seeds and plant your crops.
4. Either dry your plants or offer them fresh to local markets.

TIPS

- You might want to start this business part-time because the crops will take some time to grow.
- There are books available in bookstores and libraries about drying and preserving herbs. Learn as much as you can about the species you'll be growing.

RESEARCH SERVICE

Start up cost: $100 (for initial advertising expenses).

Equipment needed: None (although having a computer with Internet access would be extremely helpful).

Every year, thousands of businesses and individuals hire independent researchers to obtain information. Suppose an author is writing a novel that takes place in New Orleans around the turn of the century. He may hire a researcher to find out what styles of furniture and clothing were popular then. Or a contractor may be planning to build an office building in a rural area and must hire a researcher to find out what types of wildlife live in the area. There are many opportunities available for researchers.

HOW TO GET STARTED

1. Advertise your services as a researcher through small classified ads in publications that are of interest to you, or make up flyers or business cards and leave them at stores and businesses.
2. When you start getting calls, find out about the project that needs to be researched and determine whether to charge your client by the hour or project. Give an estimate.
3. Having a home computer with Internet access is invaluable in the research business, but not mandatory. If you don't have one and want to start this type of business, you should work toward getting such a system, especially if you want to operate from your home. If you don't yet have a computer or can't afford one, you can do most of your research at the library. Where you obtain your information

will vary from project to project. For example, if you're researching the eating habits of the African fire ant, visit the local university's entomology department; or if you're researching music of the 1940s, visit a vintage record store and talk to the owner. It will vary according to the subject being researched.

RESIDENTIAL FLYER DISTRIBUTION

Start up cost: $50.

Equipment needed: An accurate road map and vehicle.

All businesses need to advertise and are always looking for new ways to reach potential customers. A flyer delivery service fills that need and is a cost-effective way for companies to get the word out about their services. Flyers can be delivered for a fraction of postal rates.

The types of businesses most likely to use flyers or brochures are service companies (for example, plumbers, carpenters, contractors) who want their message to get to home owners in the neighborhood.

HOW TO GET STARTED

1. Sit down with a road map and decide your company's delivery areas. The best response from flyers will come from middle- to upper-class residential homes.

2. Walk each neighborhood and count the number of homes in the area. You will need to tell your clients how many homes can be delivered to in any particular neighborhood so that they can order the correct number of flyers for each delivery.

3. Have the client get his or her flyer designed and printed.

4. Charge the customer at a per flyer rate (currently rates are between 8¢ and 15¢ per flyer).

5. Pick up the flyers and pass them out to homes in the neighborhood. Flyers are usually left on the door step or in a plastic doorknob bag. Homes with no soliciting or no trespassing signs should be passed by. Also, it is illegal to deliver flyers or other nonmail articles in the mailbox.

TIPS

- Flyers can also be passed out on the street or placed on the windshields of cars.
- Research your local city ordinances regarding flyers.

OTHER IDEAS

- You can increase your business and offer your clients discount rates by "piggy backing" flyers. Piggy backing is when you deliver flyers for several clients at once. If you have your own business you want to advertise, you can piggy back your own flyers along with others and get free advertising. *A flyer service is a great second company.*
- If you're the creative type, you can also get into consulting and designing effective flyers for your clients. It also wouldn't be a bad idea to get friendly with a local printer. They'll be willing to give you amazing deals if you bring them enough business.

ROADSIDE SELLING

Start up cost: $50 on up (depending on what you sell) and a bit of savvy.

Equipment needed: Vehicle, poster board, and markers (for signs).

Roadside sales are hot, hot, hot! Many people are making small fortunes in this business. Let me tell you about some roadside vendors I know and the secrets of their success.

I have a friend who quit his regular nine-to-five job and is making twice as much money now selling roadside only one day a week! His secret? A hot product and a great location. This friend lives in the city and did a little research in the art business. He found a company that sells mass-produced framed oil paintings. He buys them in bulk at an incredibly low price. Every Saturday he drives out into the desert and displays his paintings at a busy gas station off of the main highway. He marks up the prices of his paintings at an average of 70 percent and sells them to tourists traveling through.

Another friend of mine wanted to make some quick money one weekend. Shortly before the Fourth of July, she remembered seeing quite a few American flags flying on homes in the neighborhood, so she picked that as her hot item. On Sunday morning she went down to the local hardware store and bought up every American flag they had for about $13 each. She made up a few large signs on poster board reading "Flags" and parked her car at the corner of a busy intersection in an affluent neighborhood. She set up four of the large flags on her car to make the display an attention grabber. Her flags sold for $35 each. Within four hours she was completely sold out and had made a profit of over $1,100!

Other good roadside items are sunglasses, toys, clothing, umbrellas, carpets, T-shirts—just about anything under the sun! Spend a little time researching the hot items and find a good location with a lot of traffic. Make up large signs with bold lettering stating what you are selling and place them in highly visible locations along the side of the road so that people will see you. You just might strike gold!

TIP

- Some cities require roadside vendors to carry a permit. Check into this before you start.

ROMANTIC DINNER CATERING

Start up cost: $400.

Equipment needed: Food supplies, cooking equipment, set of nice dishes, set of nice glasses and wine glasses, nice silverware, candles, candle holders, tablecloths, cloth napkins, napkin rings, serving dishes and serving utensils, tin foil, plastic wrap, plastic crates to transport food and dishes.

If you love to cook and can make a nice dinner for two, this could be the business you've been looking for. Romantic dinners by candle light are no longer something we see only in the movies. The service you'll be providing is a dream come true for all of those starry-eyed romantics out there who either can't cook or don't have the time to. Your clients will range from bachelors and bachelorettes to couples celebrating anniversaries who want to show their loved ones just how much they care. With this business, you'll be preparing dinner and setting up a beautiful table for the couple, usually beforehand.

HOW TO GET STARTED

1. Make up a menu of several dishes that you can offer. You can either prepare them at home and deliver them or prepare them at your client's home.
2. Have a wine list available with alcoholic and non-alcoholic selections available.
3. Have several sets of nice dinnerware, silverware, glasses, tablecloths, candle holders, and candles that your

clients can choose from. I suggest having an antique-looking setup and something more modern to choose from.

4. When taking orders from your clients, have a price list handy and give them the total price in advance, including all food costs and delivery.

5. When you arrive at a client's home, set up the table and place the food either in the oven or in the refrigerator (depending on the dish) and tell them in what order to serve things.

6. Arrange to pick up your dishes, candles, and table-cloths the next day.

TIPS

- For an extra fee, serve dinner to your clients.
- You'll probably be particularly busy around Valentine's Day, so be prepared for the extra business.
- Buy a book on the subject of etiquette and table settings. You'll want everything to be perfect.

SECURITY WINDOW
BAR INSTALLATION

Start up cost: $200.

Equipment needed: Ladder, electric drill with regular and masonry bits, hammer, masonry anchors, one-way screws, standard tool kit, and an assortment of nuts and bolts.

Installing security window bars can beautify a home as well as protect it from burglars. Iron security bars come in many shapes, sizes, and designs from very plain to ornamental with intricate detail. Many manufacturers now carry iron guards with fire release bars, which is an added safety feature in case of an emergency. Security bars are valued for their strength and beauty and can be installed on both residential and commercial properties.

I recommend starting your business by installing ready-made security bars rather then welding them yourself. You can find a huge selection of ready-made bars at an iron shop or by ordering a manufacturer's catalog. Check the Yellow Pages for shops in your neighborhood.

In most cases, window bars are installed on the outside of the house over the windows. The bars are usually screwed into the sides of the window frame using one-way screws along with the proper type of masonry or wood anchor. Measure each window dimension carefully before ordering bars for a customer.

Carry a picture book with you of different bar styles when giving a customer an estimate. This will allow you to go ahead and set up an installation appointment after the customer has chosen the type of bars he or she would like installed.

TIP

- Check with your local fire department for regulations regarding installation.

OTHER IDEAS

- Iron window bars can be painted. You might offer a painting service for an extra charge so that the bars blend in with the color of the customer's home.

SHOE SHINING STAND

Start up cost: $300.

Equipment needed: Comfortable chairs, wooden boxes (to use as foot stools), an assortment of different colored shoe polishes, saddle soap, horse hair brushes, shoe glue, leather dye, shoe shining cloths, rags, plastic foot/sock protector inserts, and a shoe buffing brush.

Old-fashioned shoe shining stands are making a comeback in a big way. One man in Los Angeles is making over $500 a day with his little stand cleverly placed in the lobby of a large office building.

HOW TO GET STARTED

1. Get your supplies together. Most of the things that you'll need are available at shoe repair stores.
2. Shining shoes is easy and can be done in just minutes. Visit a shoe shining stand in your area and have your shoes shined by a pro. Watch what he does and ask questions. The basic procedure is this: Dust off the shoes first with a rag and then with a horse hair brush. Insert the plastic protectors just inside the shoe to prevent getting polish on your customer's socks. Apply saddle soap with a rag and wipe off. Apply shoe polish with a brush and let dry. Wipe off shoe polish with polishing rag using back and forth movements until the shoe shines. Lightly apply a matching leather dye to the sides of the soles to refresh their original color.

3. Decide what building lobby you'd like to have your stand in. Pick one that has a lot of foot traffic. Contact the building manager and set up a rental contract. Another good location for a shoe shining stand is outside of a car wash where people have to stand around for at least ten minutes while waiting for their vehicles.

OTHER IDEAS

- To make your stand a success, make it look neat and attractive. Choose nice, comfortable chairs for your customers to sit in. You should consider placing the chairs up on a platform to save your back from strain. Get permission to hang a sign near your stand so customers don't pass you by. Post your prices as well.
- Have an assortment of shoe laces and non-skid sole attachments available for sale. You might even consider selling dress socks and nylons!
- Always keep a "tip" jar near your work station because shoe shiners are commonly given an extra gratuity fee.
- Make your stand personal and pleasant. You might want to have magazines or the daily paper available for your clients. Have a radio near your station broadcasting sporting events or old-fashioned music.

SOAP MAKING

Start up cost: $200.

Equipment needed: Soap molds, oils, soap coloring, soap fragrance oil, lye, pH kit, protective clothing, cellophane wrap, labels, and cooking utensils.

Soap making is a very old craft that's enjoying a resurgence in popularity. With the heavily fragranced and sometimes harsh soaps on the market today, many people are going back to basics and buying all-natural soaps. Soap making is fun and anyone can set up shop at home. A bar of soap may cost 10¢ to make and can be sold from $1 to $4! By adding special herbs, fragrances, and colors, you can make gourmet and specialty soaps right in your own kitchen. There are many different sizes and shapes of soap molds available through soap making suppliers that will make your final product more appealing.

HOW TO GET STARTED

1. There are many books available about soap making complete with recipes and lists of material suppliers. They can be found at some craft stores or by special order from your local bookstore. Soap making is a fun, easy, and profitable business that can be started on a part-time basis. Generally, soaps are made from water, vegetable oils, and lye, all commonly found ingredients. As with any craft, practice makes perfect, so always test your batches before selling them.

2. Once you've made your soaps, wrap them with a thick, clear cellophane wrap. Have some attractive labels made up

listing your company name, address, and the ingredients used. Take them to local merchants or sell them by mail order.

OTHER IDEAS

- Soaps make wonderful gifts. See the section on "Gift Baskets" for an added selling avenue.
- Make special soaps to fill a particular need, such as a gardener's soap made with cornmeal for added scrubbing power, which could be sold in local nurseries, or a hunter's soap scented with pine oil, which could be sold at sporting goods stores.

TRAVELING NOTARY PUBLIC

Start up cost: $300 (varies from state to state).

Equipment needed: State-issued notary license, bond, notary journal, and notary stamp.

You can create a nice business for yourself by becoming a notary public. A notary public is a person licensed by the state who holds the legal power to witness the signing of documents. Notaries are in great demand, especially those who can travel, to witness signings of deeds, wills, insurance policies, birth affidavits, bills of sale, and any written agreement.

HOW TO GET STARTED

1. Look in your phone book under "Notaries" and find an organization that will assist you through the process of becoming a notary. They will usually offer a seminar or class that will cover the legal aspects of becoming a notary and prepare you for your state's written exam.

2. After passing the exam, you'll need to purchase a bond and a notary journal (for record keeping) and will be issued a notary seal.

TREE TRIMMING AND SURGERY

Start up cost: $400.

Equipment needed: Extension ladder, vehicle equipped to carry ladder and tree branches, chain saw, hedge clippers with extension attachment, mallet, chisel, latex paint, and paint brushes.

Tree trimming is the perfect profession for anyone who loved climbing trees as a kid and isn't afraid of heights. Trees play an important role in our lives by producing oxygen, providing shade, and contributing their aesthetic beauty. Trees, like other living things, need to be maintained and require professional pruning, and, in some cases, surgery.

Before you begin working on trees it is very important to learn about and understand our green friends. Tree work is very precise and requires a knowledgeable professional to care for a tree properly. There are many books about tree trimming and surgery available at the library and bookstores. This chapter will give you a brief look at the very broad subject of tree care.

BASIC TREE TRIMMING

Trimming is a technique to thin out branches for shape, aesthetics, or to correct growth problems such as top heaviness or leaning. Trimming is done by removing dead branches and shaping the tree so that it can grow in its natural shape.

Removing Branches

Whether you are removing branches because they are dead, diseased, or are making the tree lean, there is a specific method used.

1. Large branches should be removed with a sharp chain saw. Cut the branch off in sections starting at the end away from the trunk. By using this method you will lessen the risk of the whole branch crashing down on the ground or falling onto and damaging other smaller branches below. It will also prevent the branch from ripping away from the trunk before you can make a clean cut. As your final cut on a branch, you will want to have only a short stump left attached to the trunk so that it is not too heavy and will allow you to properly saw it off. Refer to a tree book for diagrams of proper tree cuts. The cut should be close to the trunk without leaving a stump, but not larger than 2 feet. Discard any rotten or infected branches.

2. Once the branch is removed you'll need to dress the wound immediately to prevent fungal infections. Use a water-based latex paint designed for outdoor use and cover the wound entirely. No matter how small the branch you remove, always apply a wound dressing.

3. Balance the tree if necessary. If you've removed a large branch from one side you may have to remove one from the other side to prevent leaning. Use your judgment.

Filling Holes and Cavities

Trees sometimes have holes or cavities in the trunk or on large branches. Such holes invite fungal infection and insects and need to be handled before the disease spreads throughout the tree.

1. Remove as much of the rotting or infected wood as possible from the hole using a mallet and chisel.

2. Coat the inside of the hole with water-based latex paint or a special antifungal tree dressing.

3. If the hole is large and has damaged the structure of the tree, you may need to fill it by packing it with mortar, cement, or a plastic material.

Tree Bracing

Branches of a tree sometimes need to be braced. In most cases this is done if a branch is in danger of falling or splitting. Bracing is generally done by attaching a metal strap around the weaker branch and securing it to a stronger one.

UPHOLSTERY CLEANING

Start up cost: $200.

Equipment needed: Wet/dry vacuum, brush attachments for vacuum, dry cleaning fluid, spot remover solution, bucket, sponges, pile brush, and towels.

Dirty and spotted upholstery can be an unpleasant eyesore. Professional upholstery cleaning is often the solution for homeowners with soiled furniture.

HOW TO CLEAN UPHOLSTERY

1. Begin by vacuuming the upholstery to remove loose dirt and hair. Be sure to get in the cracks and under the cushions. Check the labels attached to the upholstery for cleaning instructions, which should tell you if the fabric needs dry cleaning or if it can be cleaned with water and a cleaning solution. If there is no label (as on antiques), go with dry cleaning to be safe.

2. Clean up spots and heavily soiled areas first. You can use a spot remover or a dry cleaning solution for this. Follow the manufacturer's instructions for the product you have chosen.

3. After the spots are removed, proceed with a full cleaning (if needed). For dry cleaning, follow the manufacturer's instructions.

Wet Cleaning

Wet cleaning refers to a solution made up of an upholstery cleaning solution and water. Test out your cleaner on a small patch to make sure that the product is right for the fabric. Make up your cleaning solution in a bucket and apply the foam by gently dabbing it on with a sponge. Water rings and stains can be avoided by not soaking the fabric and by cleaning an entire section of fabric at once. Use your wet/dry vacuum or a towel to remove excess moisture. Brush the fabric in one direction with a pile brush and let it dry.

VENDING
MACHINES

Start up cost: $500 on up (depending on what type of machines you initially purchase).

Equipment needed: Vending machines and desired stock.

You see them everywhere from gas stations and gyms to supermarkets and Laundromats. They are vending machines and people are crazy about them. Whether selling sodas, snacks, gum balls, or laundry detergent, vending machines turn other people's pocket change into your profit. Most business owners welcome vending machines in their offices and establishments because they provide their employees and customers with fresh snacks and cold drinks, making everyone happier. You can start your vending machine business with just one machine placed in a busy location. You will soon be making enough profit to buy more.

HOW TO GET STARTED

1. Look in the Yellow Pages under "Vending Machines." Call the manufacturers listed and ask them to send you their catalogs.
2. Before buying or leasing a vending machine, decide where you would like to place it. Talk to the owners or managers of ideal locations and work out a contract with them to place your machine on their property. You will be responsible for the maintenance and stocking of your machine.
3. Stock your machine and visit it about once a week. Remove the change and make sure it is working properly. Restock all items.

4. If you're selling snack items or sodas, you can buy your stock cheaply by shopping at warehouse stores.

OTHER IDEAS

- If you have your own office, consider getting a vending machine for your own employees and customers to make some extra profit.
- Video games and virtual reality machines are similar to vending machines and are more popular than ever.
- You can purchase pay washers and dryers to place in apartment buildings that aren't equipped with laundry facilities.

VIDEOTAPING SERVICE

Start up cost: $600.

Equipment needed: Video camera, tripod, blank videotapes, lighting kit, and two videocassette recorders (for editing).

These days you're not likely to find a wedding or party without someone standing by recording the event with a video camera. Video is a standard way of capturing special moments and can be a lucrative business for the professional armed with a good camera.

Many people like to hire professionals to do the taping because they know the final product will be good and they are often reluctant to ask a friend or relative to videotape the event rather than join in on the fun.

HOW TO TAPE AN EVENT

1. Go over with your client exactly what they want to capture on video. For example, a bride and groom may want you to tape their guests arriving, the ceremony, and then the reception. Everyone's needs will be different.

2. Whenever possible visit the taping location beforehand. Find out if there is an adequate power supply and whether or not you will have to bring in any special lighting equipment. Decide where the best place will be for you to set up your equipment.

3. Tape the event, capturing as much of it as you can. A shot of Aunt Edna might not seem important to you, but it could mean a lot to your clients. When in doubt, shoot it. You can always edit it out later.

4. If your client has paid you to edit the videotape as well, do so by using your two videocassette recorders. Your owner's manual will give you exact instructions on editing and making copies of tapes.

TIPS

- Learn about the subject of videotaping. Start by reading your owner's manual and get familiar with all of the features and options on your camera. You can also find books about video cameras in the library and at bookstores.
- Practice. The only way that you'll ever become a professional is to polish your skills until they're perfect.

VINYL REPAIR

Start up cost: $50.

Equipment needed: Vinyl cleaner, razor blades or sharp knife, cleaning cloths, masking tape, vinyl conditioner, and vinyl repair kit (kits are available at automotive and hardware stores). Kit should include: vinyl repair compound, patches (in assorted grain patterns), backing paper, application spatula, and paint set.

Vinyl is a plastic material that has many common uses in our world from automobile upholstery to flooring. Unfortunately, vinyl doesn't last forever. In time, harsh weather and regular wear and tear break down vinyl, causing tears and rips in the material. Vinyl repair is big business for the savvy repairman with the know-how and proper tools. Work is easy to find in this business. Just go to any restaurant or gym with vinyl upholstered booths or equipment, or take a look into almost any older car and you're sure to find torn vinyl that can be repaired quickly and easily.

HOW TO REPAIR VINYL

Vinyl repair kits can be purchased inexpensively at any automotive or hardware store. These do-it-yourself kits come with complete instructions and most of the tools that you will need. Vinyl can also be repaired with a heat process, but the simple adhesive type kits are just as effective.

1. Clean the area you will be repairing with a special cleaner made just for vinyl. Wipe the excess cleaner off with a clean cloth. Don't use oils or abrasive cleaners on vinyl because they will dry it out and create further damage.

2. With a razor blade or knife, trim off any frays, ragged edges, or burned material.

3. From your vinyl repair kit, cut a piece of backing fabric to cover the tear and insert it on the back side of the tear or hole.

4. From your repair kit, mix the paint to match the color of the vinyl. Test the color by applying a small amount on the vinyl in an inconspicuous place. When the color is right, mix up the repair compound with a spatula and add the color compound. Apply the colored repair compound to the damaged area with a spatula and wipe away any excess. Let the compound dry and apply a second coat.

5. From your repair kit, select a patch with a closely matching grain and place it directly over the filled-in tear or hole. Gently press the grain patch down and tape it in place. Allow it to dry for several hours.

6. When the compound is dry, peel away the grain patch. If the repair is not filled completely, reapply the compound and repeat the above step.

7. When the repair is complete, treat the vinyl with a vinyl conditioner to protect it.

WEATHER-PROOFING HOMES

Start up cost: $300.

Equipment needed: Ladder, garden sprayer, paint brushes, roller brush and tray, and wood sealer.

Many homes are built out of natural wood because of its beauty. Unfortunately, if the wood isn't sealed properly it will quickly fall prone to bacteria, cracking, and weather damage. Stucco and tile are also prone to water damage and staining due to their porous surfaces. All of these surfaces should be sealed. Sealing surfaces makes them waterproof and prevents costly damage to the home.

Sealing a home is similar to the process of painting a home and can be a profitable business.

HOW TO GET STARTED

1. Go to your local hardware store or painting supplier and educate yourself on the different brands of waterproofing sealers. Many of the manufacturers have brochures available about their products and offer instructional pamphlets with usage guidelines. You can also find books on painting at the library.

2. Get your supplies together and begin advertising your services. It would be a good idea to send your card to local general contractors, particularly those who specialize in new home construction. You could also leave your card at the doorstep of homes built out of natural wood.

OTHER IDEAS

- Other areas of the home that can be weather-proofed
  are fences, stucco, concrete, masonry, wooden roof shin-
  gles, decks, brick, and canvas.

WEDDING CONSULTANT

Start up cost: $200.

Equipment needed: Books about wedding etiquette and planning.

Getting married is one of the most important and special occasions in a person's life. The wedding day is one to be cherished and remembered for a lifetime. Naturally, everyone wants his or her wedding to be perfect, but without proper planning the special day often turns into a disaster. Helping couples plan and organize their weddings to ensure that the big day goes smoothly is the job of the consultant. From ordering flowers to making honeymoon arrangements, there are hundreds of things that need to be pulled together to make the event work. Some of the things that a wedding consultant may help with are flowers, music, wedding cake, favors, transportation, hotel accommodations, tuxedos, bridesmaid dresses, color schemes, themes, location, catering, decorations, and following wedding traditions if the clients wish.

HOW TO GET STARTED

1. Buy several books about wedding planning and traditions. They are available in the reference section in most bookstores. There are books available for do-it-yourself wedding planning that will be helpful. Also, buy the current issues of the bride magazines.

2. Find out where weddings are held in your area and visit them. Your clients might need ideas for a place to get married.

3. You can find clients by advertising in the phone book or by leaving your business cards at bridal shops. Wedding conventions are held in some cities and are a great place for you to have a booth to attract new clients.

4. When you have clients, meet with them, discuss their budget, wedding date, honeymoon plans, and the type of wedding that they'd like to have. Have them pay you your fee in advance and begin the planning.

5. Take some photos of the weddings you've planned to build a portfolio and generate future business.

WINDOW BOARD-UPS

Start up cost: $300.

Equipment needed: Vehicle equipped to carry large sheets of plywood and ladder, hammer, nails, ladder, electric drill with regular and masonry bits, electric saw, one-way screws, heavy work gloves, glass cutter, and masking tape.

In most cases, window board-ups are needed by business owners in emergencies, such as after a break-in or a fire. Boarding up is a temporary solution to prevent further damage until new glass can be installed, which sometimes takes days or even weeks.

HOW TO GET STARTED

1. Get your tool kit together and have a good supply of thick plywood panels and various other wood pieces.

2. Inspect the broken glass. If the window is only cracked or has only minor damage, ask the owner if he would like it removed. He may want to have it repaired instead of replaced. If the damage is not repairable, begin removing the glass. Be sure to wear a pair of heavy work gloves to avoid injury and have a trash can nearby in which to deposit the glass pieces. Gently pull shards free. If the glass is only cracked, but the owner wants it removed, gently press strips of heavy masking tape across the pane in a large criss-cross pattern. Cut around the perimeter of the pane with a glass cutter. Gently tap the at the cut lines. The glass should break away in pieces held together by the tape. Note: for large windows you should use a large sheet of adhesive material to cover the glass before removal.

3. Cut a piece of plywood to fit over the window. Your piece should overlap the window and be anchored into the window frame if possible. If the frame is unsturdy, mount the wood so that you can drill it into the exterior of the outside wall using a screw every 12 inches or so to ensure a snug fit. Use one-way screws so that the wood can't be removed by intruders.

OTHER IDEAS

- Get free advertising in the board-up business by painting the name and telephone number of your company right on the plywood panels.
- Be prepared to take emergency calls in the middle of the night as that is the time most break-ins occur. Having a few droplights for night work is helpful.

WINDOW WASHING

Start up cost: $200.

Equipment needed: High-pressure sprayer, squeegee with extension poles, ladder, vinegar, industrial-strength window cleaner, spray bottle, nylon scrub brush, and newspaper.

Why is it that no one wants to clean windows? Window cleaning can be a time consuming and tedious task for the amatuer. But for the professional with the right equipment and know-how, it can be an easy and profitable business to run.

HOW TO CLEAN WINDOWS

1. Remove the screen (if there is one). Clean away dirt from the screen with a cleaning detergent and scrub brush, rinse thoroughly, and let dry.
2. Rinse off any caked-on dirt from the window.
3. Spray the glass with a solution of vinegar and water.
4. Dry off the glass with crumpled newspaper, making sure to leave no streaks.
5. Reinstall the screen and clean the next window.

For High-up or Hard-to-Reach Windows

1. Use your high-pressure sprayer filled with window cleaning solution to wet the surface and rinse away dirt.
2. Scrub the window with the spongy side of your squeegee.

3. Clear away extra water with the rubber blade of the squeegee. With a little practice you should be able to do this without leaving streaks on the glass.

TIP

- All of the materials you need can be purchased at a janitorial supply house or a hardware store.

WINDSHIELD REPAIR

Start up cost: $50.

Equipment needed: Glass cleaner, clean cloths, and windshield repair kit (kits include repair compound and application syringe).

A cracked windshield doesn't always have to be replaced. There are many windshield and glass repair kits available that can be purchased inexpensively at most hardware or automotive stores. Windshields with minor cracks and pock marks can be fixed if the damage is not serious. This will save the car owner a great deal of money.

Each repair kit varies in materials and directions. Follow the manufacturer's instructions and guidelines, which are included in all kits.

HOW TO DO A BASIC WINDSHIELD REPAIR

1. Clean the glass thoroughly on the inside and outside with a glass cleaning product and clean cloth. Make sure that the surface is free of dust, dirt, and moisture before you begin.

2. Place a cloth below the area of the windshield that you are going to repair. The compound could damage the paint if any spills on it.

3. Fill the crack or hole with glass repair compound following the manufacturer's instructions. Make sure that there are no bubbles in the compound. Clean up any excess with glass cleaner.

4. Let the compound cure according the manufacturer's instructions.

YARD
MAINTENANCE

Start up cost: $300.

Equipment needed: Lawn mower, hedge clippers, weed trimmer, broom, rake, heavy work gloves, and trash bags.

If you enjoy working outdoors, a yard maintenance business may be the perfect profession for you. Many homeowners are too busy or dislike working in their yards. A bimonthly route to such homes for routine maintenance will be welcomed by such people.

FIVE STEPS TO EASY YARD CARE

1. Mow the lawn. (A power mower will make your work fast and easy.) Push the mower over the grass in straight lines working your way back and forth until all of the grass is evenly cut.
2. Trim or pull any weeds or patches of grass that the mower did not reach so that the job is complete.
3. Trim hedges and plants with your clippers.
4. Rake up all grass clippings, leaves, and branches. Sweep the clippings into a pile and put them in trash bags.
5. Sweep walkways, sidewalks, and porches.

TIPS

- You may want to charge an extra fee for the first visit (especially if the yard is a jungle and needs extra attention).

- Read about the subject of gardening and landscaping. There are many books available at bookstores and the library.

OTHER IDEAS

- In this type of business you can plant flowers or shrubbery for an extra fee.
- Most yards need to be fertilized at least once a year. You can easily provide this service for an additional fee.

Organizing Your New Business

Without organization the world would be a very chaotic place. Imagine a major intersection with no traffic lights. Without those lights signaling drivers to stop or go there would be a great number of accidents. Without organization in the business world, there would be a great number of bankrupt companies. Organization is establishing order through placing people and things in their proper place. To survive in business, one needs to be organized. In this chapter we will go over some of the vitally important areas of organization needed for a new company.

KEEPING FILES

When starting a new business you will undoubtedly collect a lot of paperwork. Hang on to all of your receipts, permits, and research data. You will probably need them in the future. Buy a filing cabinet and plenty of filing folders and make up clearly marked folders for each type of document. Alphabetize your files and keep them updated. For example, receipts for supplies bought to start up your business should be in their own folder—from the vacuum cleaner to the new home computer. Your business license should go in another, and so on. Think of your filing cabinet as the center of your business.

JOB RECEIPTS

Always keep a record of every job you do for a customer. The easiest way to do this is by using a three-part invoice form. The form should have a space for the date; customer's name, address, and phone number; and a section that lists what services or products were bought and the price. Your customers will expect a receipt when they pay you for your services. Give the customer the top copy (usually white) as his receipt and keep the yellow and pink copies for your records. Create a filing cabinet for the yellow copies. Make up a folder for each customer and organize them alphabetically by the customer's last name. Keep all of the pink receipts in date order in a separate file so that you have the information at hand when it comes time to file your taxes.

The yellow copies will become your client database. The information contained in those files can be a gold mine of future jobs. A satisfied customer is likely to use you again. Send regular mailings to these folks and you'll be amazed at the response rate. For information on how to send a mailing, refer to the Miniature Mailing House listing in this book.

Three-part invoice forms can be purchased at an office supply store or you can order custom forms from a printer with your company name and logo on them.

KEEPING TRACK OF YOUR BUSINESS

When you start a new business you'll want to keep track of your profit. At the end of every week, total up all of the income generated by the business (less the cost of materials) and mark it down on a sheet. As the weeks go by you'll be able to see how your company is doing by looking at the sheet. By keeping this statistic it will be easier for you to set and reach your financial goals. If you have a computer you can purchase software that will graph it out for you or you can simply do it by hand on a piece of graph paper. It would be wise to keep other statistics also, such as the number of jobs completed or the dollar amount of sales. Figure out what the main purpose of your company is and what statistics mirror your growth.

Advertising and Promoting Your Business

Advertising is simply telling people about your services and products in a way that makes them want to buy them. Promotion is the act of popularizing your service through advertising. These two go hand in hand. For example, if you've got a great product, but no ones knows about it, your chances of selling it are slim. The more you advertise, the more business you will generate. This is a tried and proven fact. With a great service or product and a clever advertising campaign, your chances of survival in business are greatly increased.

EFFECTIVE METHODS OF ADVERTISING

There are many forms of advertising available to the small-business owner. In this chapter, we will go over some of the most successful and creative forms of advertising for your new company.

Flyers

A flyer is a piece of paper with a simple message on it about your services or product. They are usually left at the doorsteps of potential customers (usually in middle- to upper-class residential neighborhoods). Flyers have proven to be one of the most cost-effective methods of advertising for small businesses. In some larger cities there are companies that will deliver flyers for you. In smaller communities there is probably no such service, which means that you will have to deliver them yourself or you can start your own flyer delivery service as a side business. See the listing in this book, Residential Flyer Distribution.

Word of Mouth

There is no better way to generate leads and jobs than by having a good reputation. For example, if you're in the bathtub refinishing business you would want all of the local plumbers to refer their customers to you. A company referred by someone that prospective customers know and trust is probably the one that they will hire to do the job. There are three ways to get other companies and people to refer work to you.

1. Contact local business owners who are in the position to refer work to you, such as a general contractor if you have a chimney cleaning company or a veterinarian if you operate a pet hotel. Tell them about your services and offer to send them some of your business cards or flyers. You might even offer them a referral fee such as a 10 percent kickback of the job price or you could agree to refer work back to them.

2. An excellent source of referrals is your customers. Every time you complete a job, ask the customer if they know of anyone that might also need your services. If they are happy with your work, chances are they'll gladly give you the names of one or two friends or neighbors. You can then contact these referrals and tell them that their friend,

Mrs. Smith, thought that they might be interested in your services.

3. Another way to turn one job into two or three jobs is by offering a "neighbor program." This occurs when you set an appointment with a customer (usually over the phone). Tell your customer that if he or she gets a neighbor to use your service while you are in the area, you will give them both a 10 percent discount. Get the names and phone numbers of neighbors and set the appointments for the same day.

Phone Solicitation

Phone solicitation is calling up potential customers and telling them about your services and products. Usually you will have a set script that you use to explain what you do and your prices. Offering some type of a discount will increase your sales. The local white pages are full of names and phone numbers. There is also a directory called the *Haines Directory* that can be found at the library. When setting up an appointment by phone solicitation, be sure to get the customer's address. The one in the phone book may not be correct or complete.

Yellow Pages

Advertising in the local Yellow Pages is a great way to be seen by new customers. Although large ads are more effective, they can be quite expensive. Check out the prices for your local directory and decide what you can afford. Being listed (even if in small print) will bring in more jobs than if you were not listed at all.

Business Cards

Having a batch of business cards printed up is a wise and cost-effective way to advertise your company. You should always give each customer one of your cards when you do a job. Most people hang on to them for future reference and may call you again in the future. You can leave a small stack of your business cards at stores, gas stations, and wherever else the owners will let you. You can also use bulletin boards at grocery stores and Laundromats.

Direct Mail

Mailing advertisements to potential customers can bring in new business. Lists of addresses can be bought from companies that specialize in mailing lists. These companies usually have the types of lists broken down into specific categories to help you target your prime candidates. You can also buy Blue Book directories which list the names and addresses of general contractors, plumbers and other professionals in the area. Take a look at the Miniature Mailing House listing in this book for more information on putting together a direct mail advertising campaign.

Previous Customers

People who have used your company in the past are the most likely to use you again. Using your old job invoices, compile a list of past customers and send them regular mailings. For example, you can send them a reminder that it is time for another cleaning or you can send them special discount coupons. Generally, your old customers will respond to your mailings and will be happy to hear from you.

Free Advertising with Press Releases

Press releases are newsworthy articles that can be sent out to the local media, such as newspapers and radio stations. You can cleverly incorporate your business into an interesting story or article and receive free advertising.

Write an article about your field of business. A good example would be a chimney sweeping company sending out an article about the dangers of chimney fires. You should include helpful hints that homeowners can use. In the article, quote yourself, "Dan Brown, owner of Classic Sweep, says, 'Chimneys should be inspected and in most cases cleaned once a year.'" Send your article to the local newspapers and be sure to include your phone number.

Getting Set Up Legally

In most cities and counties throughout the United States it is necessary to have a business license, certain permits, and insurance in order to operate legally. Before you start a company, thoroughly research what type of permits and licenses you will need for your particular city, county, and state. The business that you choose to start may also require a special license.

Please note that the estimated start up cost that you have seen at the beginning of each business listing does not include the cost of permits and licenses because the prices vary.

The following is a list of some of the different types of permits and licenses that you may need to get for your business.

SELLER'S PERMIT

A seller's permit is necessary if you are selling taxable merchandise or taxable services. The purpose of this permit is to ensure that you pay and charge sales taxes. Contact your state board of equalization for forms and more information.

CITY BUSINESS LICENSE

Some cities require you to have a license to do business within the city. In most states, you will need such a license to open up a company bank account. Once you have paid for your license you will need to have a "Doing Business As" (DBA) published in a local newspaper within a few days of getting your license. The statement lets people know who you are and the business name under which you are operating. Contact your local city hall for more information.

INSURANCE POLICIES

You may be required to carry automobile insurance on company vehicles for your type of business. You may also need to purchase an insurance policy for your actual business to protect you and your customers in the case of an accident, damaged property, theft, or any number of other reasons. If you have employees working for you it is required that you carry a workman's compensation insurance policy. Contact an insurance broker or attorney to find out what type of insurance you are required to have.

STATE CONTRACTOR'S LICENSE

Your type of business may require you to carry a contractor's license, which is issued by the state. Contact your state contractor's licensing board to find out if you will need one.

FEDERAL AND STATE INCOME TAXES

All states require businesses to file state and federal income taxes. Contact your state tax board and federal tax board to find out what forms you will need to file and at what time of the year your taxes are due. You should contact a certified public accountant for advice.

It would be wise to contact an attorney and an accountant as well as all of the organizations listed above to find out exactly what is needed to set up your business legally. Starting off with all of the correct licenses, permits, and insurance policies will save you a great deal of trouble down the road.*

*The foregoing information is not intended to be legal advice or a statement of all the legal requirements for starting a business. Readers are advised to contact an attorney as to the particular legal requirements for starting a business in their particular area. *Ed.*

How to Be Your Own Boss

WORKING ALONE

As with many small businesses, you sometimes have to start out as a one-man or one-woman show. The experience can provide you with a great sense of freedom and self-worth. You're the boss now and in business for yourself. It may be a dream come true or you may be experiencing feelings of fear and anxiety about the future. This chapter is designed to get you through the rough beginning.

SETTING A SCHEDULE

Keeping a regular schedule is important when you are working for yourself. As with working for someone else you are expected to arrive and leave at a certain time every day. Expect no less from yourself. Decide what hours your business will be open and what time it will close and follow the schedule. Don't get into the habit of bending your own rules.

MAKING LISTS

At the end of every day take a moment to look at what needs to be accomplished tomorrow. Write down all of the things that you must do. Putting these things in writing will free up your attention and allow you to concentrate. Set goals and targets for yourself and do your best to attain them. When making a list, always keep in mind the main goals that you would like to achieve with your business and work toward them every day. As you complete each task on your list, cross it off and go onto the next.

COVERING YOURSELF

There may be times when you need to leave the office during business hours. To ensure that your incoming calls are handled, either have a friend answer the phone for you or turn on your answering machine. Your answering machine should say something like, "Hello. You've reached Bob's Carpet Cleaning. We're out in the field right now or on the other line. Your call is important to us, so please leave a message with your name and phone number and we'll call you back shortly." By using the term "we" instead of "I" on your recording, your company will appear bigger and more established to the customer.

You may also want to carry a pager. You can buy one from a pager dealer and get an operating number in one day. Always wear it when you are away from your phone. With a pager you can add something like this to your answering machine recording, "We're out in the field right now or on the other line. Please leave your name and phone number or if you need immediate service, please call (your pager number) and your call will be returned within thirty minutes." Always check your messages every half-hour and return your pages immediately.

WORDS TO REMEMBER

- *Persistence*. Persistence means refusing to give up. Run your new business on a steady path, determined to reach your goals.
- *Integrity*. Integrity is the quality of being honest and trustworthy. Always charge fair prices for your services and do the best job that you possibly can. Deliver what you've promised to the customer.

THE GOOD NEWS

If you can make it through the first few weeks or months by yourself while continuing to build your business, you'll soon be able to hire employees to help you run the company. You might also consider starting your company with a partner who shares a similar interest in the type of business you are starting. A friend or relative you can trust and depend on would be a good candidate for a partner.

Selling Your Business

STARTING AND SELLING BUSINESSES AS A BUSINESS

Usually we think of selling a business as something done only when a company is in financial trouble or the owner can no longer handle the operation. This is not always the case. There are many men and women who successfully start and sell businesses *as a business* in order to turn a profit. There is nothing more enticing to a prospective business buyer than a turn-key operation at a fair price. Turn-key is a term that refers to a business that is currently operating and ready to turn over to a new owner. With a turn-key company, the owner sells the business and its assets to a new owner who immediately takes over the operation.

Businesses of all types and sizes are on the market for sale, from major corporations to small service-oriented companies. You can start a small company, get it up and running, and sell it to a buyer at a profit based on its net value and future potential.

HOW TO START AND SELL A BUSINESS

1. Start a business using one of the ideas in this book or one of your own.

2. Get it set up legally, operating smoothly, and turning a profit.

3. Based on your financial records, determine what the business is worth by figuring out what the average yearly profits were. Add in the worth of your company assets such as vehicles, equipment, computers, etc. Your asking price should be based on your hard assets, rate of growth, the length of time the business has been established, and any other economic or social trends that would indicate future growth, demand, or need for the business.

4. Advertise your business for sale either by placing an ad in the classified section of the newspaper or by taking it to a business broker. (Business brokers are specialists in the buying and selling of businesses and operate like real estate agencies.)

TIPS

- The personal interest of your potential buyer can also greatly effect the sale price of your business.
- To learn more about selling businesses, there are many good books available on the subject at bookstores or libraries. You can also seek advice from a business broker.

The Golden Rules of Professionalism

Every successful company has a set of standards and operating procedures that keep it at the top. Common sense and good manners will help you build goodwill and trust with your customers and community. Here are ten rules of professionalism:

1. Always deliver the product or service that was promised on time and at a fair price.
2. Never tell the customer that you can deliver something if you don't honestly feel that you can.
3. Always dress for success. This means wearing the proper attire for your profession and making sure that you and your employees look neat and well groomed.
4. Keep your equipment clean and in good working order.
5. Never say bad things about your competition. Concentrate on the good points of your service or product and communicate those to the customer.
6. Always handle customer problems as a priority.
7. Be polite and courteous—even to the most difficult customers.
8. Always be on time for your appointments.

9. Never do anything illegal or unethical. Hard work and integrity will lead to success.

10. Always keep your files and paperwork organized.

By following these rules you will earn a great reputation and find your work more satisfying.